# RELIGIOUS BELIEF

# CONTEMPORARY PHILOSOPHY

*General Editor*
Max Black, Cornell University

*Editorial Committee*
Charles A. Baylis, Duke University
William Frankena, University of Michigan
Morton White, Harvard University

# RELIGIOUS BELIEF

## By C. B. Martin

SENIOR LECTURER IN PHILOSOPHY

UNIVERSITY OF ADELAIDE

*Cornell University Press*

ITHACA, NEW YORK

This work has been brought to publication with the
assistance of a grant from the Ford Foundation.

PRINTED IN THE UNITED STATES OF AMERICA BY THE

VAIL-BALLOU PRESS, INC., BINGHAMTON, NEW YORK

# Preface

THERE will be no attempt in this book to talk about religious belief in general. This would almost certainly be a foolhardy enterprise. Religions differ, and it would require an intimate acquaintance with them all to be able to say what they have in common. I shall discuss those forms of Christianity which I myself have lived through or lived close to, and my comments will be relevant to features essential to these.

My method will usually be two-sided. I shall try to set out as clearly as possible what I believe to be some of the most important difficulties and confusions in religious forms of argument and assertion; then I shall give accounts of what such forms of argument and assertion might mean that would be safe from philosophical censure.

My remarks cannot be addressed to those who rejoice in contradiction as evidence of the limitations of human reason. I can only invite them to reflect that their method can be employed to populate heaven not only with God the Perfect

# Preface

Good but also with the square that is round and with a sun that is bright and always dark.

There will be those who will complain, whenever anything is shown in a clear light, that seen clearly it is no longer what they saw in darkness. For those who place value upon obscurantism, I have no argument.

## ACKNOWLEDGMENTS

I wish to thank the editors of the *Australasian Journal of Philosophy* and *Mind* for permitting me to use parts of articles first published in those journals (in Chapters Three, Four, and Five) and the Student Christian Movement Press Limited for the use of the same material, which was published in A. G. N. Flew and A. MacIntyre, editors, *New Essays in Philosophical Theology*, 1955.

Also I wish to thank the following for permission to quote: Burns, Oates & Washbourne Ltd and Benziger Brothers, Inc., from *Summa Theologica* by St. Thomas Aquinas; Routledge & Kegan Paul Ltd, from *Mental Acts* by P. T. Geach; Thomas Nelson and Sons Ltd, from Hume's *Dialogues Concerning Natural Religion*, edited by Norman Kemp Smith; Basil Blackwell, publisher, and John Wisdom, author, from *Philosophy and Psychoanalysis* and from *Other Minds*; Macmillan & Co. Ltd and St. Martin's Press, from *Essays in Conceptual Analysis*, edited by A. G. N. Flew; the editor, *Aristotelian Society Proceedings*, 1957, from "Personal Identity and Individuation" by B. A. O. Williams; and the editors of *Philosophy, The Philosophical Quarterly*, and *Australasian Journal of Philosophy*, excerpts from articles by W. D. Glasgow, H. D. Lewis, and R. N. Smart.

I am greatly indebted to Mr. B. H. Medlin, Professor D. A. T.

# Preface

Gasking, Professor J. J. C. Smart, Professor K. E. M. Baier, Mr. B. S. Benjamin, Mr. C. F. Presley, and Professor Max Black, who most painstakingly read the manuscript and made many helpful suggestions.

C. B. MARTIN

*University of Adelaide*
*December 1958*

# Contents

# RELIGIOUS BELIEF

# One

# Learning to Talk of God

A child must be taught how to talk about chairs and tables, and he must be taught how to talk about God. When he grows older, he does not, even occasionally, find that he and others have been misled and muddled in their talk about chairs and tables, but he may claim this, and with reason, concerning talk about God. When, as a child, he asks, "Who made God?" he is made to feel that he does not understand the august meaning of the things he is taught to say. When he is older, he is still made to feel that the meaning is beyond his understanding. It is as if what one means is not one's own doing but is a quality to be taken sometimes on faith.

When it is suggested that "God loves us" and the tone of voice indicates that this is a matter of great importance, the child wants to know about this person called "God" and the special nature of his love. It is difficult for the teacher to answer when the child asks perfectly naturally, "Who is God?". No simple procedure can satisfactorily settle the question in the way in which so many questions can be settled; the teacher cannot point to something, draw a picture, or do anything of the sort, without cheating. To point heavenward and say, "He lives up there and watches over all of us all the time," would be dishonest, for "God is a Spirit, and they that worship him must worship him in spirit and in truth." Of course, it will not be clear to the child or indeed to the teacher just what a spirit is. And if the child becomes frightened by the idea of an All-seeing Spirit (as children sometimes do), one cannot reassure him as one did with the giants and the fairies by saying, "It is just pretend."

Evasion and obscurity are present from the beginning. This is important, because this is usually not the case with statements undergoing philosophical analysis. Statements about material objects and pains, mathematical statements, scientific statements, and moral statements, are not (typically at least) themselves in conceptual disorder, though philosophical accounts of them regularly are. There may be a temptation to think that religious statements at their rock bottom are in order. I do not believe this is the case. At least, I do not believe it is the case with religious statements of the sort I was taught or of the sort that deserve the very general classification "Christian."

However, pictures and straightforward descriptions do seem to have a place. Pictures have been drawn of Christ which may or may not approximately represent him, and descriptions have been offered which may or may not fit him. He was visible and tangible. The child is taught about the life and work of Jesus: of his love for children, the wonderful things he was able to do, and of his heroic death. The child understands all of this, and so when it is said, "God loves us as Jesus loves us," there seems to be no evasion and no obscurity. Jesus was a man, and it makes sense to say that his love exceeded that of any other man. Then it is said that Jesus is the Son of God the Father,

## Learning to Talk of God

and the child is not quite sure what this means, but the reality of Jesus remains. Then it is added that Jesus *is* God. For God is three persons in one nature. This the child is not expected to understand, and, if he is to avoid heresy, neither is the teacher. It is defined as a mystery. The child is encouraged to attempt to believe more than he can understand. We shall examine the nature of this task in a later chapter. What is important for us to see at this stage is that the child is thus engaged from the beginning of his religious instruction.

Despite the sophistications of his teacher the child will have a rather literal idea of God in mind. He is encouraged to have this idea by many things that form his religious instruction and activity. He will see pictures of a bearded, muscular God. He is told that God can see and hear him, so it is natural that he should think that God has eyes and ears. Much of what he reads in the Bible, recites in creeds and other verbal forms of ritual, and sings in hymns has the literal form of description. He has the material for qualification without end.

Blessed art thou O Lord, Who beholdest the deep and sittest on the Cherubim. V. Blessed art Thou, O Lord, in the firmament of heaven, and worthy of praise for ever. [The Gradual]

. . . when my soul shall appear before Thee, and shall see for the first time the immortal brightness of Thy Majesty. . . . [Resolutions of the Sick]

I know that my Redeemer liveth, and that he shall stand at the latter day upon the earth. And though after my skin worms destroy this body, yet in my flesh shall I see God: Whom I shall see for myself and mine eyes shall behold, and not another. [The Order for the Burial of the Dead, *The Book of Common Prayer*]

When rising from the bed of death
O'erwhelmed with guilt and fear,

3

# Religious Belief

I see my Maker face to face,
O how shall I appear? [Addison, *The English Hymnal*]

When theologians speak of God they are anxious to deny him physical attributes. Yet theists assert and atheists deny that there is a Being called God who created the world, watches over men, knows their actions, hears their prayers, cares for their needs, speaks in the whirlwind, took upon himself flesh and walked upon earth and was seen and heard and felt. Many of the things that are said of God are strongly reminiscent of things that we say of our fellow creatures, whose physical reality we would not dream of denying. Further, their physical reality is relevant to what we say of them. We would not say that a friend heard us, provided for our needs, spoke to us, witnessed our actions, if we had no way of seeing, hearing, feeling him doing these things. Theologians tell us that it is necessary to speak of God "analogically" and that we must not take the analogies to hold strictly. Unfortunately they are not altogether helpful in telling us just where the analogies are to hold and where they are not.

There have been times when things were simpler and more clear-cut. God was visible for all to see. One need not worship him in spirit, for he was quite literally in the heavens beyond the clouds—he was the sun.

Some theologians, like Paley, have likened the action of God upon the world to that of a watchmaker upon a watch. As we find evidence of a maker in a watch, so do we find evidence of the Maker in the world. Some philosophers, like Kant, have accepted the analogy and argument but made the qualification that it did not prove all that we want to say of God, for example, that he is perfectly good. Other philosophers, like Russell, have said that the evidence at best was inconclusive and at worst was not for a good Creator but for a capricious and

4

even Satanic one. The reaction of other theologians like Barth, that such analogy and argument is blasphemous, seems nearer the truth, for this analogizing makes God like what he cannot be. Indeed, it makes him like a discernible object. That is, the analogy suggests that God is a superhuman physical agent who by physical means gives shape to the raw material of the world. The concept of God is made too clear for comfort.

One is told that of course one will not see God face to face as we now see one another, because God is a Spirit and so has not a body. How then shall we "see"? The method is that of giving a description that seems to have a perfectly straight-forward meaning and then to deny that it has that meaning without giving instruction as to what sort of meaning it has. It is as if one could give meaning to a statement by uttering a form of words and then denying all accounts (save those that leave it a mystery) of what the meaning might be. The picture that the literal form of description suggests is what remains constant as one spends a lifetime rejecting it. The child and the sophisticated theologian agree on the picture to be denied, and it may be thought that therefore they share a meaning.

Yet this is a gross oversimplification and a caricature. It is not *simply* that all suggestions as to just what it would be to "see" God are rejected.

Consider the case of a man who claims to see an evil demon and who also claims this demon to be invisible even to him. We shall be hard put to understand him. We ask if he means to suggest that he hears the demon or sees evidence of its presence, a shadow, a stir of the curtains, or that perhaps he feels the evil presence, and an awful image comes before his mind. He denies it all and, what is more, save for the expression of this claim, no difference is made in the way he lives. He does not walk in fear.

How different is the case of the religious man who sings of

seeing the face of the invisible God! For he may often feel himself in the presence of someone invisible who commands him to live a certain kind of life, to love his neighbor, to worship, to pray. The Christian is engaged in a life of verbal and nonverbal activity with but little need of examining the character of the assertions he makes and suggests by that activity. There are quite explicit directions for how he should live and speak, for what he should do and say. It is no small thing that he has for authority generations of men and centuries-old institutions, but of course he is taught that the real authority comes from God. We shall ask what this means. I shall ask for the meaning of utterances that most of us have learned to employ in childhood. My task is to examine certain key theological concepts and not to pass judgment on the moral validity of a way of life.

# *Two*

# Rationalist Substitutes
# for Religion

THE time is now past when philosophers could feel justified in dismissing religious language as "nonsense" and "meaningless." This time of brashness and idol-smashing was well spent, but it is past. There is still left the task of examining as sympathetically and as critically as possible just *how* religious utterances are used to mean whatever they may mean. Sympathy can, however, be misguided and misused. In an effort to make coherent sense of religious statements a philosopher may characterize these statements in terms of only one aspect of their use at the expense of others that are in conflict with it or that seem to be confused. This, if it is not set out clearly for what it is, is a presumption and, in any case, an evasion. It is the philosopher's primary responsibility to give an account of the more typical uses of religious language. He evades this responsibility when he isolates and makes aseptic some harm-

7

less specimen of use with the suggestion that this use, because it is harmless and not entirely useless, is what the meaning of religious statements *really* comes to. (We shall come to see in the course of argument that religious statements mean in many very different ways. It is not that they mean too little but that they mean too much. For their sorts of meaning are often incompatible.) I shall give two examples of what I take to be philosophical evasion of this kind.

First, there has been an account of the use of religious language in terms of "attitude toward life" and "behavior policy" involving no reference to the world as it really is. Religious language, in this sense, would be used rather than nonreligious language just because it had certain psychological and behavioral effects. If it were found that a nonreligious language could be substituted and yet bring about these effects, then such a language would be substituted or, at least, would be considered substitutable. The position is approximated in certain extreme forms of Quakerism.

Those who hold such a position as this might use any or all of the religious statements used by a religious believer who held that these statements were in *some* sense literally true. However, the use would be utterly different. For convenience, let us call the person holding the nonliteral interpretation the subjectivist.

When the subjectivist talks in terms of "God's will" or "the call of Christ," he may refuse to have these phrases and others like them translated into phrases not containing the words "God" or "Christ" or their equivalents ("Jehovah," "Gott," "Jesus," "Lord"). His refusal to translate them in such a way is of a peculiar sort. He perhaps refuses the Freudian's accounts ("father figure" and the like) because they cannot (psychologically) do the job that the specifically Christian phrases and statements do. When the subjectivist prays and attends church services, he does so because of the effect that such things have. He refuses to give up these religious practices for the psychoanalyst's couch just because recourse to the psychoanalyst's couch cannot do the job that the specifically Christian acts of prayer and church worship do.

The job that the subjectivist wants done is of a moral nature. He may have learned his notion of what ought to be done in many ways—at his mother's knee or from the example of the life of Christ as set out in the Bible. But, no matter what the process of learning may have been, he believes that the nature of the job is best described in Christian terms and that the employment of Christian language and practices is the best way of getting the job done. Someone might say that it could be described in terms of feelings, but this would not be so. The job is not merely a certain way of feeling best described in religious terms; it is also a mission—a vocation, a moral vocation. What the detailed nature of this vocation is may vary from one person to another. The vocation may be described as a "Christlike life or "agapeistic behavior." Attending to Biblical stories would be considered important, but it is not thought important or necessary that these stories should be considered to be true.

The clearest exposition of religious language in terms of this kind of use is by Prof. R. B. Braithwaite in his Eddington Memorial Lecture, *An Empiricist's View of the Nature of Religious Belief*. Braithwaite says,

The kernel for an empiricist of the problem of the nature of religious belief is to explain, in empirical terms, how a religious statement is used by a man who asserts it in order to express his religious conviction.[1]

---

[1] The Ninth Arthur Stanley Eddington Memorial Lecture (Cambridge: Cambridge University Press, 1955). The passages quoted below are on pages 11, 12–13, 16, and 23–25.

## Religious Belief

If by explaining "in empirical terms" Braithwaite means that the explanation itself should be free of philosophical confusion, then he is right, but from this it does not follow that *what* is explained should be free of confusion. Braithwaite leads us to expect an analysis of religious statements as they are most typically used and then proceeds to isolate a use that, though involving no confusion, is very seldom found in such isolation. Indeed, he is telling us how he and perhaps a very small minority use religious statements. His account is almost a legislation as to how religious statements should be used most harmlessly and profitably rather than a description of the rich confusion of uses that typify religious language as it is used by those who assert the existence of a perfectly good and powerful Creator whose nature is beyond our understanding and whose judgment we may fear.

Because Braithwaite believes that religious assertions are fundamentally moral assertions, he begins by giving an analysis of moral statements. Concerning the man making a moral assertion,

what is primary is his intention to perform the action when the occasion for it arises. . . . A utilitarian, for example, in asserting that he ought to act so as to maximize happiness, is thereby declaring his intention to act, to the best of his ability, in accordance with the policy of utilitarianism.

It is perhaps unfair to criticize an analysis that so unavoidably suffers from the limitations of space, but qualifications or elaborations seem crucially necessary. The man who says, "I know what I ought to do here, and I intend, to the best of my ability, to avoid doing it," does not obviously contradict himself. Braithwaite goes on to say that

the meaning of a religious assertion is given by its use in expressing the asserter's intention to follow a specified policy of behaviour.

## Rationalist Substitutes

This policy is described as "an agapeistic way of life," which is explained in terms of most of the thirteenth chapter of First Corinthians.

The other important component is that certain stories should be reflected upon (though not necessarily believed) for the psychological aid that such reflection would be to successful "agapeistic behavior."

On the assumption that the ways of life advocated by Christianity and by Buddhism are essentially the same, it will be the fact that the intention to follow this way of life is associated in the mind of a Christian with thinking of one set of stories (the Christian stories) while it is associated in the mind of a Buddhist with thinking of another set of stories (the Buddhist stories) which enables a Christian assertion to be distinguished from a Buddhist one. . . . For it is not necessary, on my view, for the asserter of a religious assertion to believe in the truth of the story involved in the assertion.

This account is clear and unconfused. It suffers only by being so nearly autobiographical. One is accustomed to expect that a religious form of words will be used to make a kind of claim about the nature of the world.

There is another use of religious language in which such a claim is made, but a weak one. I shall call it pseudopantheism. According to this view religious statements are used to emphasize and organize certain features of the world. Thus, these statements can be true or false, profound or shallow, but they make no reference to anything over and above the world.

For instance, the statement "God is Creator and Judge, merciful and righteous" would be a means of cosmic simplification. Many features that we had not related together would be related in a kind of pattern. Innumerable instances of goodness unexpectedly being rewarded and evil being punished would be related. So many things in nature would be seen to have the

11

look of things kindly devised that we might feel less fear. All this and much more could be accomplished by the pseudo-pantheistic use of the statement. Of course, what would be accomplished would *not* be a reference to a particular Being above other beings. It is because of this lack that I cannot take it seriously as a use of religious utterances.

Even when a philosopher (for example, Prof. John Wisdom in his article "Gods") employs and describes such a use with subtlety and grace, he is no ally to the faithful. A pseudo-pantheist is a kind of atheist, for he finds the theist's assertions to be muddled or false or a mixture of the two. The pseudo-pantheistic reductions have, however, a subtle force of argument. After they are provided, the theist must answer the forbidding question "What more?"

It is of interest to see how Wisdom's argument in "Gods" can be read as a profound development and correction of Hume's masterpiece, the *Dialogues Concerning Natural Religion*. Perhaps it is because this piece of subtle and ingenious irony is such a sublime work of high comedy that it has never been seriously considered by religious thinkers. The whole is so artfully conceived that any quotation or summary must be inadequate if not actually misleading. I shall quote only the segments of argument that relate to Wisdom's thesis.

But there is a species of controversy, which, from the very nature of language and of human ideas, is involved in perpetual ambiguity, and can never, by any precaution or any definitions, be able to reach a reasonable certainty or precision. These are the controversies concerning the degrees of any quality or circumstance. Men may argue to all eternity, whether HANNIBAL be a great, or a very great, or a superlatively great man, what degree of beauty CLEOPATRA possessed, what epithet of praise LIVY or THUCYDIDES is entitled to, without bringing the controversy to any determination. The disputants may here agree in their sense, and differ in their terms, or *vice versa;* yet never be able to define their terms, so as to enter into each other's meaning: Because the degrees of these qualities are not, like quantity or number, susceptible of any exact mensuration, which may be the standard in the controversy. That the dispute concerning Theism is of this nature, and consequently is merely verbal, or perhaps, if possible, still more incurably ambiguous, will appear upon the slightest enquiry.²

Here, Hume suggests an analogy that Wisdom works out in detail. Hume makes it look as if, when two disputants know all the facts about Hannibal's biography and continue to dispute as to his greatness, their dispute must be "merely verbal" and, consequently, trivial. Wisdom is at pains to point out how such a controversy can be nonverbal, important, and rational.

*Suppose two people are looking at a picture or natural scene.* One says "Excellent" or "Beautiful" or "Divine"; the other says, "I don't see it." He means he doesn't see the beauty. And this reminds us of how we felt the theist accuse the atheist of blindness and the atheist accuse the theist of seeing what isn't there. And yet surely each sees what the other sees. It isn't that one can see part of the picture which the other can't see. So the difference is in a sense not one as to the facts. And so it cannot be removed by the one disputant discovering to the other what so far he hasn't seen. It isn't that the one sees the picture in a different light and so, as we might say, sees a different picture. Consequently the differences between them cannot be resolved by putting the picture in a different light. And yet surely this is just what can be done by talk perhaps. To settle a dispute as to whether a piece of music is good or better than another we listen again, with a picture we look again. Someone perhaps points to emphasize certain features and we see it in a different light. . . . Besides running over in a special way the features of the picture, tracing the rhythms, making sure that this and that are not only seen

---

² N. Kemp Smith, ed., *Hume's Dialogues concerning Natural Religion* (London: Thomas Nelson and Sons, 1947), pp. 217–218.

but noticed, and their relation to each other—besides all this— there are other things we can do to justify our attitude and alter that of the man who cannot see. For features of the picture may be brought out by setting beside it other pictures; just as the merits of an argument may be brought out, proved, by setting beside it other arguments, in which striking but irrelevant features are emphasized; just as the merits and demerits of a line of action may be brought out by setting beside it other actions.[3]

Hume takes a step himself toward showing how a non-factual difference may be an other than verbal difference. In the following he sees how in such a case the disputants may sort out different facts for emphasis and organization.

It seems evident, that the dispute between the sceptics and dogmatists is entirely verbal, or at least regards only the degrees of doubt and assurance, which we ought to indulge with regard to all reasoning: And such disputes are commonly at the bottom, verbal, and admit not of any precise determination. No philosophical dogmatist denies, that there are difficulties both with regard to the senses and to all science: and that these difficulties are in a regular, logical method, absolutely insolveable. No sceptic denies, that we lie under an absolute necessity, notwithstanding these difficulties, of thinking, and believing, and reasoning with regard to all kind of subjects, and even of frequently assenting with confidence and security. The only difference then, between these sects, if they merit that name, is, that the sceptic, from habit, caprice, or inclination, insists most on the difficulties; the dogmatist, for like reasons, on the necessity.[4]

Hume leads the atheist to accept the sort of emphasis upon and organization of the facts that has been mainly the theist's

---

[3] John Wisdom, *Philosophy and Psycho-analysis* (Oxford: Basil Blackwell, 1953), pp. 158–160.

[4] Smith, ed., *Hume's Dialogues*, p. 219 n.

prerogative. This bloodletting and meaning-exhausting technique, found in gentler form in "Gods," is the final irony of the *Dialogues*.

I ask the Theist, if he does not allow, that there is a great and immeasurable, because incomprehensible, difference between the human and the divine mind: The more pious he is, the more readily will he assent to the affirmative, and the more will he be disposed to magnify the difference: He will even assert, that the difference is of a nature which cannot be too much magnified. I next turn to the Atheist, who, I assert, is only nominally so, and can never possibly be in earnest: and I ask him, whether, from the coherence and apparent sympathy in all the parts of this world, there be not a certain degree of analogy among all the operations of Nature, in every situation and in every age; whether the rotting of a turnip, the generation of an animal, and the structure of human thought be not energies that probably bear some remote analogy to each other: It is impossible he can deny it: he will readily acknowledge it. Having obtained this concession, I push him still farther in his retreat; and I ask him, if it be not possible, that the principle which first arranged, and still maintains order in this universe, bears not also some remote inconceivable analogy to the other operations of Nature, and among the rest to the economy of human mind and thought. However reluctant, he must give his assent. Where then, cry I to both these antagonists, is the subject of your dispute? [5]

If one thinks of theism as mainly a certain organization of facts about the world and not as a reference to some kind of ultimate Being outside of the world and our comprehension, then atheists and theists may be led gently to agreement. Who can deny "that the cause or causes of order in the universe probably bear some remote analogy to human intelligence"? [6]

---

[5] *Ibid.*, p. 218.      [6] *Ibid.*, p. 227.

15

# Religious Belief

For, as Hume says in another place,

*that nature does nothing in vain,* is a maxim established in all the schools, merely from the contemplation of the works of nature, without any religious purpose. . . . One great foundation of the COPERNICAN system is the maxim, *that nature acts by the simplest methods, and chooses the most proper means to any end:* and astronomers often, without thinking of it, lay this strong foundation of piety and religion.[7]

If the organization of such facts is theism, then there will be few atheists, just as from Wisdom's analysis it would seem that few sensitive and intelligent men would be atheists for long when they realized that theism asserted nothing in the least outrageous.

This sort of pseudopantheistic reduction does not analyze the medley of uses typically given to religious forms of utterance but presents an account of a substitute use so aseptic that it can make "theists" of us all. But then there will be left the job of analyzing the statements of those who refuse such a reduction and will have none of this substitute. Among these will number nearly all the religious thinkers in the Christian tradition and the vast majority of those who have made Christian belief and practice a part of their lives. Considering only the problem of what to select and what to neglect, such a task is enormous, but it is this task with which the remainder of this book has to deal.

[7] *Ibid.,* p. 214.

# Three

# The Perfect Goodness of God, I

WE are taught from childhood to praise God in word and action. The ritual forms of sacrifice arc laid down for us. We learn to think of God as the only fit object of such praise and worship. The stories of God's action in history as related in the Bible inform us as to the praiseworthy qualities of God. Yet such stories tend to make these qualities different only in degree from the qualities of men. The religious impulse is to make the qualities of the object of worship different somehow in kind from the qualities of his creatures. It is part of the act of praise to put God's goodness and power beyond the compass of human understanding. It is also in praise of God to speak of him being as he is by a necessity not possible in men. I shall try to show how such a way of thinking of God can lead to difficulties.

In this and the next chapter we shall examine a number of assertions that are commonly made concerning God—that he is perfectly good, that he is not only good but the source of all moral value, that he is necessarily good. Each of these contentions, it will be argued, turns out on closer examination to be logically incoherent. Finally, we shall consider the typically Christian claim that the logical difficulties of non-Christian theism are resolved by the notion of Christ the God incarnate, the Mediator between God and man.

God, we are told, is our Heavenly Father. Like an earthly father, he watches over us, is wise and loving and good. But this analogy, though it may help us to understand, must not, we are told, be pressed too far. The goodness of God is somehow different in kind from that of his creatures. For God's goodness is perfect beyond the compass of human understanding. But we may wonder whether this account is adequate. For if, on the one hand, God's goodness is not ultimately like that of an earthly father, how does our understanding of the latter help us to grasp the goodness of God? If, on the other hand, we retain in our conception of God something of the idea of a good human father, we are left with a notion which, while a perfectly comprehensible one, is a merely human one that falls short of the divine perfection. The account does not seem satisfactory. The trouble is that it gives with one hand only to take away with the other and nevertheless leaves us with the impression that we still have something in our hands. In the course of my argument I shall try to present a possible positive account of God's unique goodness that is not in conceptual disorder. Those theologians who will reject it will have the task of adding to it or replacing it with something other than confusion and evasion.

In order to demonstrate all this it will be necessary to enter rather fully into the kind of analogy by which we are invited to talk of God. To bring it home to ourselves we shall have to treat it in as concrete and vivid a way as we can.

# Perfect Goodness of God, I

## I

Let us imagine conversations of the following sorts.

### Case A

MARY: "What *ought* we to do about Mother? We've thought and thought about it and there just doesn't seem any way to decide."

JANE: "I don't know what is the right thing to do."

MARY: "How I wish Father were still alive. He would know."

JANE: "Somehow he always seemed to know what was right."

### Case B

MARY: "Even though Father is gone, I feel that I have to do what is right just because that is what he wants."

JANE: "I know what you mean. That feeling is even stronger than when he was alive."

MARY: "Yes, and if I didn't know that he was somehow there I don't think that anything would matter."

### Case C

BETTY: "But I don't see why I ought to do this and not that."

MOTHER: "Because Father says so—that's why."

The use of "will of God" is like and unlike the use of "Father" in the three cases above. I shall talk about these cases in themselves and then relate them to theological cases.

### Case A

Mary and Jane (for whom Father is indeed a "father figure") have tried to reach a moral decision, and because the choice is a very complex one and there is no obvious way in which to decide, they feel at a loss. They remember Father's superior moral vision and wish that he were there to help them make the decision, because "he always seemed to know what was right." Time after time they found that his decisions were wiser than theirs. They had good reason, were justified, in trusting him.

*19*

# Religious Belief

## Case B

Mary and Jane remark that since Father's death they have come more and more to feel compelled to do what is right because that is what he wants them to do. It is not just that they feel they ought to behave in certain ways now because if he were alive that is how he *would* want them to behave. It is more than that. The strength of this compulsion comes from their belief that in some sense he still, even now, wants them to behave in this way. Their allegiance is to Father dead yet somehow alive. The unseen guiding hand and the unheard approval or disapproval are more powerful than the seen and heard. They also feel as if the difference between doing right and not doing right would not matter or concern them if they didn't believe that Father still wanted them to do right. "What is right" has become (by induction) closely tied up with "What Father wants us to do." The tie-up has come about by induction because Father has so often been right: they might give as a reason "Father says so" or "Father wants us to do this." This would be a good or bad reason just insofar as Father has shown himself wise in the past about moral issues. After his death, they still want to have this reason ("Father says so" or "Father wants us to do this"), though, of course, they no longer can hear his judgment.

## Case C

Betty is objecting that she sees no reason why she should do one thing and not another. Mother's answer ("Because Father says so—that's why") is supposed to provide that reason. If this answer is interpreted quite literally and Betty is intelligent, she will answer, "But that isn't any reason at all. Father's saying so doesn't make it right." Mother's answer, however, is not meant literally. It may mean a number of things such as the following. "You ought to obey Father." "Do as you are told." "There isn't any particular reason why, except that Father wants you to do it."

These three cases must now be related to theological cases. God is totally different from Father. The difference will come out as each case is examined.

### Case A

Mary and Jane feel in need of justification for choosing one alternative instead of another in a difficult moral choice before them. Father could have provided that justification because his decisions had always proved wise; therefore, his judgment would have amounted to justification.

The situation is different with theologians and God. Justification, by means of reference to God, is sought not only for difficult ethical judgments ("Pacifism is right") but also for obvious ethical judgments ("Lying is wrong"): indeed, all ethical statements equally require justification of this sort. The justification must be peculiarly general. It will be seen later what the nature of its generality is.

The nature of the justification in terms of "Father says so" or "Father wants us to do this" depends upon the success and failure of Father's judgment in the past. The nature of the justification in terms of "It is the will of God" does not depend upon the success and failure of God's judgment in the past, because God is defined as perfect. God cannot be wrong, so investigations as to whether he is right or wrong are irrelevant. If God is perfect, then nothing *could* count as evidence against his rightness. If anything *could* count as evidence against his rightness, then the justification of ethical statements in terms of God's will is not absolute.

### Case B

In this case Father is as close to God as he can be. He is dead. The authority of the dead and the authority of God are secure in ways not possible for the living, whose judgments are spoken unmistakably out of their mouths, yet there is all the difference. In a way, statements about Father dead are no closer in their logic (in their use) to statements about God than are statements about Father alive. With Father dead, he seems more infallible than ever. Mary and Jane have the glowing memory of his wisdom, and he is no longer around to be wrong. When (for example, in dreams) Father now makes known to them his judgment, they test whether it was really Father who "spoke" to them by the wisdom and success of the judgment. If it proves unwise, then it could not have been Father. If it proves wise, then it was Father, and they have something of the reason they had for a moral decision when he was alive. They have Father's wisdom of the past and his saying something is right or wrong. Father's "speaking" in dreams is like God "speaking" in prayer. In both cases neither can "speak" evil counsel, for then it would not really be Father in the dream or God in the prayer, it would just seem so. It almost seems that Father has been deified.

Imagine that Mary and Jane dreamed that Father spoke to them saying, "You ought to tell Mother of your plans for marriage, for she must be encouraged to live her life according to new patterns. Protecting her as you have done only makes her lack courage." They might, on the basis of this dream, think they ought to do this, because it is what Father says to do. They will be struck by the similarity of the moral wisdom of Father in the dream with the moral wisdom of Father when alive. Imagine, however, that they dreamed that Father spoke to them saying, "Have no scruples about lying; take advantage of others or they will take advantage of you." They would not, on the basis of this dream, think they ought to do this, because it is what Father says to do. They will be so struck by the dissimilarity of the evil counsel of Father in the dream with the

moral wisdom of Father when alive that they will not count
this counsel as coming in any way from Father. Something
like this could happen even in the case of the first dream. Say
that they accept the counsel of Father in the first dream as
coming in some way from Father and act in accordance with it.
Circumstances which should have been anticipated then prove
the counsel to have been foolish. They would then say that it
could not have come from Father though it seemed at the time
to do so. How well the wisdom and rightness of Father dead
are protected! How strong the faith of the daughters! But it is
only when nothing *could* count against their confidence that it
is of a logical sort.

Now, what if Father's diary were found by Mary and Jane
some time after his death? In Father's handwriting are accounts of the most evil deeds and descriptions of how he has
been exploiting the trust of his wife and daughters all through
the years. Evil maxims are laid down as the rules by which he
lived. Further still, it comes out that Father had committed
bigamy. The daughters are shocked and disillusioned beyond
description. Their faith and confidence in Father are completely destroyed, and never again will they give as reason for the
rightness of an action that "Father says so" or "Father wants us
to do it." Losing this reason, which had seemed so admirable
and sure in the past, may seem like losing *all* reason for judging
between right and wrong. *This feeling of ethical defeatism
would be inconsistent, however. Mary and Jane are able to
judge between right and wrong apart from what Father says
and wants, because their final disillusionment comes as a result
of judging as wrong what Father says and wants.* Yet, something very precious and certain has been shown to be paste and
false. The loss may well be demoralizing.

We have seen how Father, even as dead, is not secure enough
from discredit for there to be a strict equivalence of "X is

right" to "Father says X is right" and "Father wants us to do X." But, of course, Father is not God. God is totally different. He is the *Ultimate* Ground and Justification of Value. It is time now to turn to the last case.

*Case C*

Betty's literal interpretation of Mother's remark works as a kind of escape from the disciplinary force and meaning of the remark. If Mother had said instead, "Father knows best," Betty could still have taken this literally by answering, "Father can be wrong like the rest of us. He doesn't know everything." Again she has avoided the disciplinary force and meaning by an obstinately literal interpretation. Mother's only recourse is to say what she has meant all along, "Do as you are told. You ought to obey Father."

Father alive or dead is fallible. He "can be wrong like the rest of us." He is not God. Just because he is fallible, can be wrong, does not know everything, he is totally different from God.[1] Finally we come to talk about God. It could not have been done without the talk about Father, for we come to know what God is by coming to know what he is not.

God is the "Ultimate Good in the form of a supreme and personal Will." God is "the perfect Good." [2] This may be put in a more formal but a misleading way in the following:

A. It is one's ethical duty to love one's neighbor as oneself.
B. It (the moral judgment expressed by A) is in accordance with the will of God.

If B is asserted, then A must also be asserted. The phrase "in accordance with the will of God" works in this way like "is valid" or "is true." If B is denied, then A must also be denied.

---

[1] There is "no possibility of error in His judgments" (Charles Gore, *Belief in God* [London: John Murray, 1921], p. 120).

[2] George Galloway, *The Philosophy of Religion* (Edinburgh: T. and T. Clark, 1920), p. 202.

## Perfect Goodness of God, I

The Good is defined in terms of God's will. Yet this is not enough, for it must be added that God's will is perfect. Being perfect, it cannot but be Good. This is how moral values are established in the ultimate constitution of things. But what have we come to? Absolute justification and absolute perfection; circularity and logical vacuity. The Good is defined in terms of God's will; God's will (as perfect) is defined in terms of the Good. Nothing in the world of fact or the world of imagination can disturb this equivalence—it rests secure in the cold and barren world of logic. No wonder we found such a difference between Father and God.

The circle must be broken. When it is asked, "What is Good?" the answer must be more than "the will of God." When it is asked, "What is the will of God?" the answer must be more than "the perfect Good." The concepts cry out for content and application. And, of course, this is supplied. "The Word was made Flesh."

There are answers to the question "What is the will of God?" other than the circular answer "the perfect Good." The Bible is the revelation of the divine will, and the life and person of Christ is the embodiment and fulfillment of that will. Answers might be, "Read the Bible, pray, and learn of Christ."

Christ lived and taught on earth. He was seen and heard by men. Some of these men came to think of him as never being wrong. His moral wisdom was shown in case after case. When we read of him, we may be struck by the consistency of his moral profundity. *But note that Christ can be credited as an instantiation of the perfect will of God only just so far as we judge him to be good.*[3] Just as Mary and Jane are able to judge between right and wrong apart from what Father says and

---

[3] The view that the concept of the incarnation helps to resolve the logical difficulties that we may raise will be considered in the last section of the next chapter.

wants, so we are able to judge between right and wrong apart from what God says and wills, for we judge his will to be good. The only oddity is that we will not *call* anything God's will if it is not good. This is because we are making a definition and not giving a description. There is *no* analogy here with Father.

That we do and must judge God's will as good makes empty the claim that somehow our moral judgments depend upon God as the Perfect Good. First we *judge* God to be good, and then we try to *define* him as good. The logical difficulties here will be discussed in the next chapter.

## II

The discussion above must now be related to what religious thinkers have actually said so that the problem of God as "the source of moral values" may be brought into sharper relief.

That God is perfectly good is common ground among theologians. Many of them, though by no means all, would go further than this. They would claim that God is not only perfectly good but also the source of all moral value. According to the *Encyclopedia of Religion and Ethics*, for instance,

In the theological systems moral law is regarded as the rule of conduct which has its ground in the nature or will of God and not in the nature of man or in the consequences involved in obedience or disobedience to the law. The rule may be for the good of man, but it is for his good because it is the divine will, and not the divine will because it is for his good.[4]

A less boldly phrased assertion is made by de Burgh.

The moral law is not, as Kant held, wholly self-imposed, but presupposes a source above the subject who acknowledges its unconditional authority.[5]

---

[4] *Encyclopedia of Religion and Ethics*, ed. by J. Hastings (Edinburgh: T. and T. Clark, 1928), p. 833.
[5] W. G. de Burgh, *From Morality to Religion* (London: MacDonald & Evans, 1938), p. 189.

# Perfect Goodness of God, I

Values have no absolute value save in God.[6]

A more official pronouncement, also, I think, rejecting the independence of ethics and theology, is the following.

If God is the loving God, whose righteous Will is the source alike of the natural order and of the moral law, as is implied by the 19th Psalm, it follows that worship must include as its most vital element the submission of our wills to the Divine Will, and that service of God can only be rendered through righteousness of life.[7]

At least at first thought (we shall give second thoughts in a later chapter) there seems to be no obscurity in the idea of God as the source of the natural order. God created the world to go according to one order of things rather than another. But even at first thought there seems to be overwhelming obscurity in the idea of God as the source of the moral law. What did God do? As source of the natural order, he made and shaped the world in a certain way. As source of the moral law, what did he do? In what follows, I shall try to disentangle several possible replies.

It might be suggested that God was not the source of the moral law by anything that he did but rather by what he is. "An absolute moral law is conceivable only on the supposition that it has its ground in an existent Being who is supremely good." [8]

Comfort may be taken in the assertion that there is "no possibility of error in His judgements," [9] and God may thus be

---

[6] *Ibid.*, p. 199.

[7] Church of England, Archbishops' Commission on Doctrine, *Doctrine in the Church of England, The Report of the Commission on Christian Doctrine Appointed by the Archbishops of Canterbury and York in 1922* (London: Society for Promoting Christian Knowledge, 1938), p. 42.

[8] G. Dawes Hicks, *The Philosophical Bases of Theism* (London: Allen & Unwin, 1937), pp. 238–239.

[9] Gore, *Belief in God*, p. 120.

made good by definition. This is an extreme view that is rarely put forward explicitly but very often implied. St. Thomas says it is a "contradiction in terms" to assert that God is able to sin.[10] This view will be discussed in detail in the next chapter.

Another explanation of how God is the source of the moral law might be that God has so made the world and organized the hereafter that by and large good is rewarded and evil punished. We may doubt that things are quite as neat as this, but it remains true that the world is not so constructed as to make attempts to live a moral life impossible. (The world could have been so constructed that in large measure only selfish activity was profitable.) Thus, to say that God is the source of the moral law would be a highly misleading way of saying that God is the source of the means by which we are able to live in accordance with the moral law. I think, however, that most theologians who would employ such a form of words would want to mean more than this. A further explanation, supplementary to the above, would be one in terms of natural law.

In the very constitution of his (man's) nature, he too has a law laid down for him, reflecting that ordination and direction of all things which is the eternal law. The rule, then, which God has prescribed for our conduct, is found in our nature itself. Those actions which conform with its tendencies, lead to our destined end, and are thereby constituted right and morally good; those at variance with our nature are wrong and immoral.[11]

How one should behave toward others depends upon their needs and their capacities—upon their natures. What one should expect of oneself depends upon one's needs and capac-

---

[10] Aquinas, *Summa Theologica* (London: Burns Oates & Washbourne), Q25, Art. 3. Benziger Brothers, Inc., publishers and copyright owners in U.S.

[11] *The Catholic Encyclopedia* (New York: Encyclopedia Press, 1910), art. on Natural Law.

ities—upon one's nature. The injunction "Know thyself" has relevance to moral endeavor. It is possible to talk of the nature of man (in contrast to the nature of dumb brutes). It is true and important to say that it is man's nature to be rational. This is something about man that divides him off from other creatures. What is more, it is relevant to moral reasoning. To prevent a man from developing his rational nature is, I think, obviously evil. A moral condemnation of Nazi Germany would be to say that Nazism did not take seriously the rational nature of man.

What is right or wrong depends upon the needs and capacities of those concerned. God created man to have the needs and capacities he has. However, this does not so far make God the source of the moral law. What has been said so far is perfectly compatible with a nontheistic moral system. The moral law would be in the form of the hypothetical, "Given capacities and needs X, then A is in general the right action, and given capacities and needs Y, then B is in general the right action." How does God figure in this? If God created us, then it would be reasonable to suppose that he knows far more concerning our needs and capacities than we ourselves know and also more concerning their satisfaction and fulfillment. It would be reasonable to place greater confidence in his moral judgment than in our own. All of this may be meant by saying that God is the source of the moral law, but I do not think even this would be all that most theologians who would employ such a form of words would want to mean by them.

A still further explanation is one in terms of God as lawgiver.

The moral law is not, as Kant held, wholly self-imposed, but presupposes a source above the subject who acknowledges its unconditional authority.[12]

---

[12] de Burgh, *From Morality*, p. 189.

# Religious Belief

Contrary to the Kantian theory that we must not acknowledge any other lawgiver than conscience, the truth is that reason as conscience is only *immediate* moral authority which we are called upon to obey, and conscience itself owes its authority to the fact that it is the mouthpiece of the Divine Will and *imperium*.[13]

There are two rules of the human will: one is proximate and homogeneous, namely human reason; the other is the first rule, namely the eternal law, which is God's reason, so to speak.[14]

Connected with the concept of God as lawgiver is the notion of God's very special authority over us. This is brought out in the following quotation from St. Thomas.

All men alike, both guilty and innocent, die the death of nature: which death of nature is inflicted by the power of God on account of original sin, according to I Kings, iii, 6 the Lord killeth and maketh alive. Consequently, by the command of God, death can be inflicted on any man, guilty or innocent, without any injustice whatever.—In like manner adultery is intercourse with another's wife, who is allotted to him by the law emanating from God. Consequently intercourse with any woman, by the same command of God, is neither adultery nor fornication.— The same applies to theft, which is the taking of another's property. For whatever is taken by the command of God, to Whom all things belong, is not taken against the will of its owner, whereas it is in this that theft consists,—Nor is it only in human things, that whatever is commanded by God is right; but also in natural things whatever is done by God, is, in some way, natural.[15]

This means that God as our creator has absolute rights over us, and so whatever he commands or wishes we are obliged to do. When we are indebted to a fellow creature, he has some right over us, and we are to some extent obliged to his will.

[13] *Ibid.*     [14] Aquinas, *Summa Theologica*, Q71, Art. 6.
[15] *Ibid.*, Q94, Art. 5.

30

Yet, it is not without qualification that the more we are indebted to another, the more right he has over us and the more we are obliged to his will, for this is true only within limits. A parent to whom a child is greatly indebted has *no more* right to injure the child merely because he gets pleasure out of doing so than has the casual acquaintance who has given the child a sweet. No matter what the degree of indebtedness, there are some things that no one has the right to do—or even more nearly the right to do—to us. Therefore, even God has no absolute right over us. Of course, you can say, "But God is different in kind from creaturely saviours and parents." It is not clear that this difference is such that he can do what he likes with us. For then he could behave like Satan, and we would have no case against him. Do we praise him then for refusing to do us constant injury, for surely we should be obliged to praise him even if he did us this injury? If God can not remain praiseworthy and do what he likes with us, then he does not have *absolute* rights over us. Or, we may put it, the act of praise is the act of judgment.

Furthermore, this whole argument seems to rest upon the principle that those to whom we are indebted have special rights over us. But whether we agree with it or not, this surely is a moral principle. Therefore, there is at least one moral principle not dependent for its validity on the divine will.

The word "law" is used in many ways. It is not always an edict. When it is used in the sense of positive law, it implies a lawgiver. The way it is used in the phrase "law of identity," however, does not imply a lawgiver. When it is used in a still different way, as in "the moral law," it also does not imply a lawgiver. *For any moral lawgiver would have to be judged as good by laws we already accept before we could respect and accept his law.*

## Religious Belief

There are theologians who would assert the independence of ethics and theology, who would deny that the objectivity of moral values was somehow dependent upon the existence of God. My remarks have not been addressed to them.

# Four

# The Perfect Goodness of God, II

MOST theologians would want to say that God's goodness and other qualities are of a very special sort. God's qualities are different in more than degree from the qualities of men. What is the nature of this difference?

St. Thomas has provided the following answer to this question.

Therefore, everything that does not imply a contradiction in terms is numbered amongst those possible things, in respect of which God is called omnipotent; whereas whatever implies contradiction does not come within the scope of divine omnipotence, because it cannot have the aspect of possibility. Hence, it is better to say such things cannot be done, than that God cannot do them. . . . To sin is to fall short of a perfect action; hence to be able to sin is to be able to fall short in action, which is repugnant to omnipotence. Therefore, it is that God cannot sin, because of His omnipotence.[1]

---

[1] Aquinas, *Summa Theologica*, Q25, Art. 3.

## Religious Belief

Sometimes we may wish to say that a man is good by a kind of necessity of his nature, and this would be a way of separating him not only from those who do evil but also even from those who may regularly do good.

A man may regularly do good in such a way that we feel that circumstances would have to have been only very slightly different and temptation only a very little stronger for him to have done evil instead of good. Such a man would not be by nature good.

A man may regularly do good in such a way that we feel that circumstances would have to have been vastly different and temptation very much stronger for him to have done evil instead of good. Such a man would be by nature good.

Finally, a man may be a complete saint (whether or not there has been such a saint is not our concern) so that he does good in such a way that we feel that, no matter how different the circumstances or how strong the temptation, he would do good and refrain from evil. Such a man would seem hardly human. We would say that he was good by a kind of necessity of his nature. Yet he would be different only in degree from the rest of us. We can conceive of what it would be like for him to err, though there is no chance of his doing so.

When St. Thomas says "to be able to sin is to be able to fall short in action, which is repugnant to omnipotence," he plays upon a hidden ambiguity. When we use the expression "to be able," we may have in mind some real degree of likelihood or we may have in mind bare logical conceivability. That I am able to persuade all my readers of the validity of my arguments is false in one sense, in that there is *no* real degree of likelihood of this, but true in the other sense, in that it is conceivable or meaningful (though false) to say that I should do so. There is *no* likelihood that I should someday find a fairy under a toadstool, though it is conceivable that I should do so. Concerning the complete saint as I have described him, there is no likelihood of his doing evil, though, of course, it is conceivable (I can describe what it would be like) that he should do evil.

If St. Thomas means the expression "to be able" to indicate that there is some degree of likelihood, then "to be able to fall short in action" is indeed "repugnant to omnipotence." But if St. Thomas means the expression "to be able" to indicate bare conceivability or meaningfulness, then "to be able to fall short in action" is *not* "repugnant to omnipotence." But this must be argued less schematically.

Imagine a conversation between Mary and James. They are discussing human frailty, and James cites an exception to the general rule and says of John, "It is his nature to be kind."

Mary answers, "Yes, but we can imagine how even John could go against his nature."

James may resist this in two ways, one natural and one unnatural. The latter is analogous to theological talk of God's nature.

The natural resistance might take the following form.

JAMES: "No, I don't think that I can imagine that John should go against his nature. It seems to me just inconceivable that John should ever do anything unkind."

MARY: "Oh, I suppose it really is terribly unlikely, but all the same we can imagine that he should have been brutal in the past or be brutal in the future."

JAMES: "Good heavens, if that is all you mean, then just because we can imagine this of John, it doesn't in the least reflect upon his character or throw any doubt on the fact that it is his nature to be kind. I thought at first that you meant by 'imagining him to be unkind' that his being unkind was somehow likely, and this just isn't true. After all, we can deny that he is unkind, has been unkind, will be unkind, and still be able to imagine what it would be like for him to be unkind, to go against his nature."

Now let us have James make the unnatural resistance to Mary's suggestion. The dialogue can begin in the same way.

JAMES: "No, I don't think that I can imagine that John should go against his nature. It seems to me just inconceivable that John should ever do anything unkind."

MARY: "Oh, I suppose it really is terribly unlikely, but all the same we can imagine that he should have been brutal in the past or be brutal in the future."

JAMES: "It isn't a matter of likely-unlikely at all. I said it was inconceivable, and that is what I meant. If he did something brutal, he wouldn't *really* be John, and even imagining brutality of him is impossible, because what you imagine couldn't apply to the real John."

Connected with this last speech of James's is a further alternative. He might have said the following:

JAMES: "It isn't a matter of likely-unlikely at all. I said it was inconceivable, and that is what I meant. I don't say that John might not do something or be imagined to do something that had the *appearance* of brutality, but whatever he does or can be imagined to do would *really* be kind no matter how it appeared."

This position of James might at first appear to be that of a man whose faith in a friend is abnormally strong. This, however, is not so and cannot be so if the case is to be analogous to the theological one. Yet, it is impossible to mark off any boundary line between unshakeable faith and logical certainty or vacuity. People do sometimes speak in vague and ill-defined ways so that we are at a loss to say just how they are using language.

The statement made by James is: "John cannot in fact or in

imagination be said to go against his nature and be unkind."
He may keep this statement logically secure in two ways, even
in the face of the strongest opposition.

MARY: "Look, let us both agree that John is in fact kind by
nature, but still it is consistent with this assertion to imagine
him to have been otherwise than he in fact is, for this imagining
doesn't affect what we say he is actually like. Though we assert
that John is by nature kind, we can imagine that he might have
been unkind, that is, have beaten his wife, starved his children,
and done all sorts of unkind things. This kind of supposing
needn't worry you, James. It doesn't in the least denigrate the
actual character of John, for this sort of thing can consistently
be said of the most angelic, perfectly blameless creature conceivable."

This comment by Mary is the strongest opposition to the
statement made by James. The two ways in which he may keep
his statement logically secure and vacuous are the following.

1. He may deny the subject. If an opposing statement made
by Mary is "John might (though he didn't) have beaten his
wife, starved his children, and so been unkind," then James
may deny that this supposition could be made of John. That is,
he will say of any such person that he cannot *really* be John.

2. He may deny the predicate. James can deny that any acts
predicated, even in supposition, of John could be called unkind.
They would only *seem* so, *appear* so.

In the first alternative James uses the word "John" not to
apply to a creature but to apply to a concept (in which case it
is used as a description). This concept or description is incompatible with the concept or description "unkind." Confusion
arises because as long as unkindness is not asserted of him, it
appears that "John" is not a concept or a form of description
but a person. It is only when the possibility of predicating unkindness in fact or in imagination of John is denied that we

discover that for James the word "John" applies to a concept or description, not to a man.[2]

In the second alternative James uses "kindness" and "unkindness" in such a way that when he predicates "kindness" of John it is not used to mark off instances of kindness from instances of unkindness. Again, this monstrous use is not discoverable when James predicates "kindness" of John when John is in fact kind. It is only when the possibility of predicating unkindness in fact or imagination of John is denied by James that we discover that James fails to mark off "kindness" from "unkindness" as applied to John and therefore leaves his statement vacuously, certainly true. Consequently it does not describe in any way the character of John though it has the form of doing so.

But, is the situation really as pure, unalloyed, and clear-cut as this account makes it appear to be? No, it is not, but from this it does not follow that the account is incorrect. The case must be examined more closely.

We have granted that John is in fact kind by nature. It has been shown how very differently James thinks of the "kindness" of John, and we have gone so far as to accuse James of using this word vacuously when he applies it to John. This accusation has not been made on impulse, it has been carefully worked out. Yet something seems not exactly right about it. It smacks of lack of sympathy and of classificationism. The statement has been fitted rather uncomfortably into a box labeled "Logically Vacuous." James may well complain. Let us hear him out.

He may say, "You fail to emphasize our agreement. We both agree that John is in fact kind by nature. If we were to write testimonials as to his character, we should not write differently. Yet you say that my statement does not really describe his

---

[2] The crudities of this characterization will be corrected at the end of this chapter.

character at all. We both use our statements to approve of John. Yet you say that my statement is logically vacuous. After you get through describing my statement, I no longer recognize it as my own. You don't seem to be aware of the possibility of a man having unlimited faith in a friend."

This is an example of how sensitive statements are to philosophical analysis. As we get more and more clear about a statement it seems to change. This is inevitable. But, unfortunately, there is more to it than this in our present case, for James's statement has not been seen clearly enough.

It is not that James talks in a completely different way from Mary about the kindness of John. *The point is rather that he talks not in one sort of way but in two ways at once.* Each way must be brought out by a different procedure. I want to suggest that there is a similarity here to theological talk about Christ. Remember, John really is kind by nature and we are allowing no doubt about this.

James speaks and acts like Mary in many ways concerning the matter of John's character. He approves heartily of him, writes testimonials, holds him up as a good example, desperately tries to imitate him, and urges his children and others to imitate him. He has faith in John in the sense that when others may doubt John's kindness he does not; he does not believe bad reports, slander, gossip. His faith is strong, but as seen from this perspective only it is not religious.

But James's "unlimited faith" has another aspect, which we have already treated in some detail. This aspect is revealed by the peculiar way in which James reacts to certain suppositions we make of John. We assert that, though John is by nature kind, he might have been different and could (though we assert he will not) be unkind in the future. This is not an attack upon John's actual character, but it *is* an attack upon James's concept of the nature or character of John. We have shown how this

39

logical security has led to logical vacuity. The "faith" of James is "ultimate" indeed.

The uneasy and impossible combination of the two ways of talking is what makes James's "faith" in John religious in kind. It embraces the identical paradox embraced by theologians in their account of the incarnate Christ. We must turn once again to God and his incarnation. The analogy must already be clear.

All seems to be well as long as the goodness of Christ is not really called in question. Theologians admit freely enough that if the goodness of Christ is in doubt then his divinity must be in doubt, and, of course, if the goodness of Christ is denied then it must also be denied that he is God. However, they think that there is nothing contradictory remaining if the goodness of Christ is asserted without qualification and he is called God, the Perfect Good. I have been at pains to point out that a contradiction of an irresoluble sort remains still. The contradiction is: Christ can be conceived to have been other (that is, not good) than he was, yet as God it should be not just false but *inconceivable* that he should have been not good. I shall return to this point at the end of this chapter.

Now let me try to put my point in a more formal and more exact way.

The term "God" may be used in either of two ways. It may be used as a proper name referring to a particular being *or* it may be used as a descriptive [3] term. I believe that the attempt to use it in both ways at once results in contradiction and that theologians (in particular, Aquinas and Anselm in the passages quoted) are so anxious to make God's goodness, knowledge, and power necessary to him in ways not possible for other beings

---

[3] An expression "describes," is "descriptive," is a "description," or is used "descriptively" when in using it one attributes a property or set of properties to something.

that they have involved themselves in this contradiction. But this account is oversimplified, and now the oversimplifications must be corrected.

1. If the term "God" is used descriptively and means something like "the eternal, all-good, all-knowing, all-powerful creator of all things," then the statement "God is good" is true by logical necessity. The statement "God is good" where "God" is used descriptively in the way indicated would come to: "The eternal, *all-good*, all-knowing, all-powerful creator of all things is good." Similarly, "gorgon" is a descriptive term. The statement "A gorgon is snake-haired" would come to: "A snake-haired woman whose look petrifies observers is snake-haired." The statements "God is good" and "A gorgon is snake-haired," where the terms "God" and "gorgon" are used descriptively and not as proper names function as meaning instructions. Part of the meaning of the descriptive term "God" is "a being that is all-good," and part of the meaning of the descriptive term "gorgon" is "a being that is snake-haired."

Consistent with the definition, one cannot without logical inconsistency apply the term "God" to a particular being and refuse to apply the term "good." It should be obvious by now that this does not mean that it is inconceivable that this being should have been other than good. The necessity refers not to the being or his nature but to our use of the terms "God" and "good." That is, since part of what we mean by the description "God" is "a being that is all-good," either we must be prepared to apply the term "good" to a being whom we describe as "God" or we use the terms inconsistently with the meaning we have laid down.

Naturally, if it turns out to be true that the being we have described as "God" does evil or the being we have described as a "gorgon" grows ordinary hair then, to be consistent with the meaning we have given to the terms, we *must* refrain from describing those beings as "God" and as a "gorgon," *or* we must change the meanings of these descriptive terms.

Now we come upon a basic difference between the logic of "God" and the logic of most other descriptive terms. It could be said that the concept "God" has an "eternal" logic and has a unique reference; that is, it can be applied to one and only one individual.

*a*) Consider the descriptive phrase "the shortest adult male on earth." This phrase may be truly applied to a particular person. Then that person, quite remarkably, begins to grow. The descriptive phrase can no longer be truly applied to that person, but it was truly applied to him in the past. This phrase can apply to one and only one person at any one time, but it can apply to different persons at different times.

*b*) Consider the descriptive term "God" (which I have roughly defined by the descriptive phrase "the eternal, all-good, all-knowing, all-powerful creator of all things"). This term can be truly applied to one and only one individual, and, in order for it to be truly applied at any time to that individual, it must be truly applicable to him for *all* time. This "eternal" application of the term "God" is different from the "eternal" reference of even the phrase "the tallest man who has ever lived or will ever live." For although this phrase must have unique application to one and only one person for all time, it does not cease to have application to him if he dies. But, if the term "God" is truly applied to a being, that being must eternally exist and eternally have the qualities of all-goodness, all-powerfulness, and so on. It is therefore inconceivable that a being truly described as "God" should at any time be truly described as not-good. However, it is in virtue of the fact that the descriptive terms "not-good" and "lacking power" are *meaningfully and falsely* applied or applicable for all time to this being that he is truly described as "God."

In summary then:

i) It is inconceivable that a being truly described as "God" (good, powerful, and so on) should be truly described as "not-good."

This just means that it is inconceivable that a being truly described as "good" should be truly described as "not-good."

ii) It is, however, conceivable that a being truly described as "God" (good, powerful, and so on) should have been (as he was not) not-good or should be (as he will not be) not-good.

This just means that it is conceivable that a being truly described as "good" could have been otherwise than he was, is, and will be, in such a way that he would have been truly described as "not-good." That, which is in fact true of this being, and on account of which the description "God" is warranted, could have been false. We know the sort of thing that this being could have done or could do which would make the description "God" false, and we deny that he did, does, or will do such things.

St. Thomas said, "To sin is to fall short of a perfect action; hence to be able to sin is to be able to fall short in action, which is repugnant to omnipotence. Therefore, it is that God cannot sin, because of His omnipotence." If the claim that "God cannot sin" comes down to (i), then it is valid. If this claim amounts to the denial of (ii), then it is not valid.

2. If the term "God" is used not descriptively but as a proper name, then it is not true that the statement "God is good" is true by logical necessity.[4] The statement "God is good" (where "God" is used as a proper name) states a matter of fact and can be asserted or denied without contradiction. Now the logical

---

[4] This will be qualified when the nature of proper names is examined.

issue seems to be perfectly straightforward. Either the term "God" is being used as a description (in which case the statement "God is good" is true by definition) or it is used as a proper name (in which case the statement "God is good" is true or false as a matter of fact and can be denied without contradiction). Confusion and contradiction arise when the term "God" is used in both ways at once. So far I have presented the matter as if it were as straightforward and as uncomplicated as this. Unfortunately, there are complications and essential refinements. It is time to bring these into the open.

It was said earlier that where the term "God" is used descriptively, the statement "God is all-good" works like a meaning instruction. That is, it tells us that part of what is meant by the word "God" is "being that is all-good."

Where the term "God" is used as a proper name, the statement "God is all-good" or the statement "God is the creator of all things" may work in ways parallel to a meaning instruction —as a naming instruction. That is, it would be part of the instruction as to what being the name is to refer.

Coming to understand the use of a name and coming to understand the use of a descriptive term are parallel in ways not often emphasized. We use a descriptive term to refer to a thing, quality, event, or process or to a set of things, qualities, events, or processes of a certain *kind* different from all other kinds. (What we are to call a "kind" will ultimately depend upon general facts of nature, our perceptual constitution, and perhaps practical considerations and an element of arbitrariness.) [5] Someone has learned to use a descriptive term when he can use it to refer to a thing or set of things of a certain kind in the way laid down by the language of which that term is a part. A child may get closer and closer to understanding the use

---

[5] Sorting out the logical complexities of this truth is an exceedingly difficult task that cannot be undertaken here.

of a descriptive term. He may first use "dog" to refer to a creature or creatures of the kind "four-footed animal," then of the kind "four-footed animal with toenails." Dogs actually are of this kind, but the term "dog" is used to refer to a certain *kind* of four-footed animal with toenails, and the child does not fully understand the use of the term until he can make this reference with the word.

We use a name to refer to one and only one individual. Someone has learned to use a name when he can use it to refer to one and only one individual. A child may get closer and closer to understanding the use of a name. He may use "Daddy" to refer to "adult male" individuals, then "adult male with beard" individuals. Daddy actually is such an individual, but the name "Daddy," when it is used as a proper name, is used to refer to one and only one such individual, and the child does not fully understand the use of the name until he can do this with the word.

It will be of help to consider here some of the ways in which we learn how to apply proper names in nontheological contexts in order to throw light on the peculiar difficulties of the name "God."

1. The most straightforward way in which to learn how to apply a proper name is by introduction to the person or by having the person pointed out. If someone says, "Let me introduce Jack Bright," or, "There is Jack Bright, third from the left," the job is done as simply as can be. One may succeed in learning the application of the name in either or both of two ways.

*a*) One may associate the name with a person uniquely marked off by a description. "Jack Bright is the chap that I met last night at the party" or "Jack Bright is the chap pointed out to me as third from the left in the receiving line."

*b*) One may associate the name with a person by a clear

memory of his physical appearance. This works well enough if he is not an identical twin.

No one would want to claim that the name "God" was learned in either of these ways. The name "God" is not learned by introduction or by having God pointed out. The name "God" is learned by description, and only after the description is mastered does one claim to have "met" God by religious experience. One is prepared for the "encounter" of religious experience by knowing what sort of being (here we would have to know a description) is to be experienced. The situation is not like that of entering a room, seeing someone unfamiliar, and on asking, "Who is that?" being told, "That is Jack Bright." I do not mean this to be a criticism, for clearly we can learn how to apply names without having been introduced to a person or without having had the person pointed out to us.

2. One can learn how to apply a name by description only. The descriptions are of these kinds.

*a*) Nonindividuating descriptions. These are descriptions that hold true of more than one person, for example, "fat, tall, contemporary of Socrates."

*b*) Practically individuating descriptions. These are descriptions that do not in fact hold true of more than one person, for example, "entrusted by Socrates with the offering of a cock to Asclepius" (this entrustment was not, but might have been, shared).

*c*) Logically individuating descriptions.[6] These are descriptions that could not, without contradiction, hold true of more than one person at one time, for example, "the closest friend of Socrates."

If I know only nonindividuating descriptions of Crito, then

---

[6] I have been informed since writing this section that the phrase "logically individuating descriptions" is also used by P. F. Strawson in his book *Individuals* (London: Methuen and Co., 1959). This is a coincidence.

I do not know how to apply the name "Crito" to one and only one individual. It could be said that my use of the name "Crito" is inadequate. It is not, however, totally useless, for, in terms of the example above, at least I should not apply the name to someone who was not a contemporary of Socrates. It does not follow that someone who knows a practically individuating description [7] of Crito, and who therefore can give a unique application of the name "Crito," knows more about Crito than someone who knows only nonindividuating descriptions.

When one refers to an individual by the name "Crito," one must know at least one description of that individual, namely "possesses the name 'Crito.'" But what sort of description is this? Obviously, it is not a description of the same kind as "possesses a bulbous nose."

There is a sense of "possessing a name" or "being called a name" that is consistent with the thing so called never having existed. Names in fiction work like this, and the figments of a child's imagination are frequently called by name.

There is another (and primary) sense of "possessing a name" that is not consistent with the thing so called never having existed. In this sense there are two ways in which something may possess a name.

1. One may have a name or a number of names that are given without one's knowledge and by which it is not expected that one shall call oneself. Names are even given to people after their death. A name possessed in this way is no very personal possession.

---

[7] One can think that one knows a practically individuating or logically individuating description and be mistaken, and therefore one's use of a name can have the form of making a unique reference even when it fails to do so. Further, one can mistake a practically individuating for a nonindividuating description, and therefore one's use of a name can have the form of not making a unique reference even when it succeeds in doing so.

2. One may have a name or a number of names that are given in such a way that it is expected that other people should be able to refer to one by that name or names *and* one should be able so to refer to oneself. In this sense a name is no inconsiderable part of one's life.

Consistent with this latter sense then, the descriptive content implied [8] by the reference "the person called Crito" (where no other description of the person is known) will be "a person who has been referred to, by himself and others, as 'Crito.'" This descriptive content will be *nonindividuating* if there has been more than one such person, or *practically individuating* if there has not been more than one such person.

Primitive peoples have frequently thought of the possession of a name as something like a magical quality. The perfectly proper suggestion made by some philosophers that names may just refer to and not describe people may mislead one into thinking that one can, almost by magic, make reference to individuals whom one can in no way describe or indicate by any method other than calling by name.[9] We have just seen how

---

[8] I mean "implied" in a loose sense and not "entailed." For this descriptive content would be largely lacking if the person named died at birth.

[9] P. T. Geach, *Mental Acts* (London: Routledge and Kegan Paul, 1957), pp. 68–69, says, "To a thing to which a general term is rightly applied, those attributes may be said to be essential which logically follow from the general term's being true of it; but no attributes logically follow from a thing's being given a proper name. (Essay, III.vi.4.). Notice that I spoke of rightly applying a general term, but not of 'rightly' giving a thing a proper name; for, on the theory I am considering, we give proper names by fiat and there is no right or wrong about the procedure. A thing is introduced to me by its proper name, and thereafter I can refer to the same thing by using that name; but the name tells one nothing about the attributes of the thing."

1. A general term is *given* by fiat as much as is a proper name. There is no reason in nature why books should have been called "books" and not "smickles." Cf. other languages. It is true that there are naming

someone who knows only the name of an individual may employ the name to make reference to that individual by means of the implied practically individuating kind of description mentioned above. If even this descriptive context were lacking the name would lose its referring function.

So far I have oversimplified the situation by speaking as if in every case one *must* be able to give a description. Obviously, this is wrong, for one may be at a loss to give a description of someone and yet be able to recognize him on meeting him. This procedure is not, however, open to us in the case of people whom we have never met.

There may be a number of separately nonindividuating descriptions that *taken together* form a practically individuating description. For example, I may know that someone called Aloysius Churchill, fat and jovial, is my contemporary, resides in Athens, Georgia, works in a post office, and in his spare time collects stamps. Clearly, taken singly, each one of these is a

---

rituals (baptisms), but there is no reason why names shouldn't just "catch on" (like nicknames) just as descriptive words do. One must not confuse how names are acquired with how they are used.

2. The comparison should not be between "rightly applying a general term" and "rightly giving a thing a proper name," but between "rightly applying a general term" and "rightly *applying* a proper name." One can wrongly apply a proper name just as one can wrongly apply a general term.

3. "A thing is introduced to me by its proper name, and thereafter I can refer to the same thing by using that name." A thing is "introduced" to me and called by a general term (in which case, I must apply the term to things similar to it) or called by a proper name (in which case, I must apply the word in a way that singles out only that thing). In neither case do I refer to a thing of that kind or to that particular thing by just uttering the word. I must be able to utter the word in the presence of things of this kind or in the presence of this particular thing. Or I must be able somehow to describe this kind of thing so as to mark it off from other kinds or to describe this particular thing so as to mark it off from other things. Otherwise, I have not learned how to apply the general term or to apply the proper name.

nonindividuating description, but taken together they may form a compound practically individuating description.

Some practically individuating descriptions are more "individuating" than others. It may be true that one and only one person saw the lights change at a usually busy intersection, but there could easily have been more. But it almost passes belief that there should have been more than one person (in this case Moses) found in the bulrushes by a member of a royal family and raised in the royal household.

A parallel point holds true of logically individuating descriptions. That someone was the shortest person in a particular room at a particular time is something that cannot be true of more than one person, but it could have been true of many. That someone was the losing commander in chief of the French forces at Waterloo is something that cannot be true of more than one person, and furthermore it could have been true of very few. And of the description "author of Hamlet" it passes all belief that this could have been true of anyone else other than the person of whom it was true, that is, that someone else also could have thought of and written down just those words.

Are there any logically individuating descriptions true of one person that could not sensibly have been true of anyone else? Clearly, someone else *could* have written Hamlet other than the person who did, though only a madman could think this a serious possibility. But what of the description "born of such and such parents at such and such time," where the time is so specific that even twins will be born at different times? This description holds true of one and only one individual, and it cannot at the same time hold true of more than one individual. But could it have held true of a different individual? The answer is "Yes" and "No." The answer is "No" if we think of actual individuals, part of whose identification is their birth at certain times of certain parents. The answer is "Yes" if we think of an individual who might have existed (and did not) and who might have been born of those parents at that time. That is, a quite different individual (for example, of different sex) might have existed of whom that particular logically individuating description was true. I cannot think of any description that holds true of a particular person in such a way that it could not have held true of at least someone else who might have existed. This, I think, is so even of God.

If I know only nonindividuating descriptions of a person, then, even if I am told a name, I cannot employ that name to refer to one and only one person. However, if I learn either a practically or logically individuating description, then I can employ that name to make a unique reference.

This analysis of proper names must now be employed in the examination of the use of the name "God."

1. We are taught the use of the name "God" by description. The descriptions tend to be all logically individuating. God is the "highest." It would indeed be blasphemy to teach the use or to use the name "God" by means of only nonindividuating and practically individuating descriptions. God is described as the *one and only* eternally all-good, all-powerful, all-knowing creator of all things. God is described as "over all others."

2. It has been said that names have a connotation as well as a denotation. This is a highly misleading thing to say, but there is some point in saying it.

Suppose that I have learnt the use of the name "Napoleon" by means of the following descriptions: (1) the second son of Charles Bonaparte and Laetitia Ramolino; (2) the losing commander in chief of the French forces at Waterloo; (3) the one and only exiled Emperor of France, who ended his days at St. Helena; (4) the captain of artillery who distinguished himself at the siege of Toulon; and (5) the officer given supreme command of the Italian Campaign in 1794. I use the name "Napoleon" to refer to that person of whom all these descriptions are true. If historians were suddenly to discover a mass of evidence indicating that a fantastic impersonation had taken place (such that the person of whom descriptions (1) and (4) were true was killed by and impersonated by another person of whom description (5) was true, who in turn was killed by and impersonated by another person of whom descriptions (2) and (3) were true), then I might say that the historical figure that I had learned by description to call by the name "Napoleon" had never existed. There was, indeed, *a* "Napoleon" (a person called "Napoleon") of whom (1) and (4) were true and *a* "Napoleon" of whom (5) was true and *a* "Napoleon" of whom (2) and (3) were true. The descriptions that were supposed to be true of one and only one person turn out, when taken together, to be true of three people. When taken separately, they are true of three people.

There are several things that I can do with my use of the proper name "Napoleon." (*a*) I can say "Napoleon" refers to that person of whom (1) and (4) are true and claim that Napoleon was never Emperor of France or exiled on St. Helena. (*b*) I can say "Napoleon" is a word that is used as three proper names to refer (by description) to three different people. (*c*) I can say that the proper name "Napoleon," as I had used it, no longer has any application and that even if I use the name "Napoleon" it will be a *different* proper name. Here, I would be counting as necessary criteria for the use of the proper name "Napoleon" (in its original application) the assertion, or at least the lack of denial, of *all* five descriptions.

The statement "We have found out that Napoleon was not Emperor of France or exiled on St. Helena or the losing commander in chief of French forces at Waterloo" will, consistent with (*a*), be considered to be true; consistent with (*b*), it will be neither true nor false but in need of rephrasing so that it will read, "Someone called Napoleon was Emperor of France and exiled on St. Helena, and someone called Napoleon was the losing commander in chief of French forces at Waterloo, and they are not one and the same person"; consistent with (*c*), it will be considered to be senseless. This would be a way of underlining the decision that the word "Napoleon" is used as a proper name referring to someone of whom *all* five descriptions are true and that if one or more of these descriptions is considered to be false the proper name becomes bereft of that reference. The word "Napoleon" may then be used as a proper name having a different reference (a reference to someone, for example, of whom only descriptions (1) and (4) are considered to be true), and this difference of reference would, consistent with (*c*), be thought to amount to the word "Napoleon" being used as a *different* proper name.

Throughout this section I have used the phrase "proper name" in a less ambiguous way than is usual.

The same word "bank" can be used to refer to things of different kinds (a river bank or a financial institution). This distinction is marked off by saying that the word can be the same and the concepts different. Similarly, the same word "Smith" can be used to refer to different individuals. This distinction I would mark by saying that the word can be the same and the proper names different. Consistent with my analysis, to say that two people have the same name is *just* to say that the same word is used to refer to them. To say, as I have just said, that even if the same word is used the proper names are different is to say that the word is used differently (for example, by means of descriptions, as already indicated) in its reference to each person. If I use a name "to refer to numbers of people," [10] then I simply have not named *anyone* or used a proper name at all. If I call out, "John Smith!" and ten people called "John Smith" come to me, it would be a joke for me to show satisfaction with the response. It would be like a person saying, "I want to go to the bank," and then being satisfied whether he is taken to the riverside *or* the financial institution.

The point may be put summarily. There are two entirely different senses of the phrase "proper name." [11]

1. A proper name (in sense one) is a word that can be used on different occasions to refer to different individuals. In this sense, two or more people may share a proper name. It is in this sense that the word "name" is used in the question "What name shall we call the baby?" Similarly, a financial institution and the side of a river share the same "name."

2. A proper name (in sense two) is the *word as it is used* (perhaps by means of description as already indicated) to refer to one and only one individual. In this sense, two or more people cannot share a proper name. Similarly, if we use the phrase "descriptive term" to mean a *word as it is used in a certain way*, then when the word "bank" is used to refer to a financial institution it is a different descriptive term [12] from when it is used to refer to the side of a river.

---

[10] The analysis of proper names that has been given in this section is opposed to the analysis given by P. F. Strawson: "Of ordinary proper names it is sometimes said that they are essentially words each of which is used to refer to just one individual. This is obviously false. Many ordinary personal names—names *par excellence*—are correctly used to refer to numbers of people" ("On Referring," reprinted in A. G. N. Flew, ed., *Essays in Conceptual Analysis* [London: Macmillan & Co., 1956], p. 47).

[11] Strawson neglects to make this particular distinction.

[12] This is an intermediate classification lying between "word" and "concept." I understand "concept" to mean roughly "the *use* to which a word may be put whatever the word may be."

It is clear that I have been talking about proper names in the second sense.

Now we are prepared to see that descriptive terms (or, if preferred, "common nouns") have logical features similar to those of proper names, and most especially do they share the features brought out in our consideration of the problems of reference of the name "Napoleon" as treated above.

Suppose that I have learnt the use of the term "whale" by means of the following descriptions: (1) the largest creature on land or in the sea; (2) a fish (water-breathing creature) that on surfacing blows clouds of moisture into the air; and (3) a creature having certain distinctive shapes. I use the term "whale" to refer to creatures of whom all these descriptions are true.

It then turns out that the creature that I have described as a fish (water-breathing) breathes air. There are several things that I can do with my use of the term "whale." (*a*) I can say "whale" refers to creatures of whom (1) and (3) are true and claim that whales are not and never were fish. (*b*) I can say that the term "whale," as I had used it, no longer has any application and that even if I use the term "whale" it will be a *different* descriptive term. Here I would be counting as necessary criteria for the use of the descriptive term "whale" (in its original application) the assertion, or at least the lack of denial, of *all* three descriptions.

The statement "We have found out that whales are not fish" will, consistent with (*a*), be considered to be true; consistent with (*b*), it will be considered to be self-contradictory. This would be a way of underlining the decision that the term "whale" is used as a descriptive term referring to something of whom *all* three descriptions are true and that if one or more of these descriptions is considered to be false the descriptive term becomes bereft of that reference. The term "whale" may then be used as a descriptive term having a different reference—a reference to things, for example, of whom only descriptions (1) and (3) are considered to be true—and this difference of reference would, consistent with (*b*), be thought to amount to the word "whale" being used as a *different* descriptive term.

Suppose that I have learned to apply the word "God" (whether as a proper name *or* as a descriptive term) by means of the following descriptions: (1) the creator of all things, (2) the one and only one all-good being, and (3) the one and only one all-powerful and all-knowing being. I use the term "God" to refer to that being of whom all these descriptions are true. If I then come to think that the being that I have described as "all-good" is not all-good, there are alternative things that I can do with my use of the term "God." (*a*) The statement "We have found out that God is not good" may be considered to be *true* if we allow "God" to be a proper name or a descriptive term that is used to refer to a being of whom descriptions (1) and (3) are true. (*b*) It will be considered to be *senseless* or *self-contradictory* if we allow "God" to be a proper name or a descriptive term that is used to refer only to a being of whom *all* three descriptions are true. Thus the supposition that one of the three descriptions is false would be considered to be a canceling out of the naming instruction or the meaning instruction (which might be marked by saying in the one case, "That is not *whom* I mean by 'God,'" or in the other case, "That is not *what* I mean by 'God'").

Therefore, after this most circuitous route we have come to see how the statement "God is good" is necessarily true when the term "God" is used as a descriptive term and, more surprisingly, how it may be in a sense necessarily true even when it is used as a proper name. But even in the latter case the necessity in no way applies to the *being* (if any) named "God."

Usually, the nature of God's goodness is not described with the clarity and precision of the description quoted from St.

## Perfect Goodness of God, II

Thomas on page 33. The following passage from *Doctrine in the Church of England* is an instance of nice obscurity.

He must be perfect Goodness, perfect Beauty, and perfect Truth. As Perfect Goodness He must be the sustainer and the goal of moral effort, such effort being taken to include all effort after Beauty, Truth, and Goodness. As Holy Love He is at once infinitely exalted and completely intimate; His holiness abases us, while His love invites us to communion. It is through some inkling of His glory that all moral effort is initiated (even in atheists), and it is in finding or rather being found of Him that both achievement and reward of such effort consist.[13]

Calvin takes a position at the opposite pole from St. Thomas. It may admit of some ambiguity but at least is not a fog of all meaning to all men. According to Calvin, men occasionally fail to do good, but God does not. God is not changeable like man, but is steadily and consistently beneficent in all things and at all times.

It would seem on Calvin's account that God is that being whose nature is such that, unlike other beings, he on no occasion does evil and can be relied upon always to do good. This means (contra St. Thomas) that the attribution of evil to God is not self-contradictory, but false and blasphemous. God is a moral giant who is in fact, but not by definition, good. It is also a matter of fact and not definition that no man is thus consistently good. If such an interpretation is allowable, there is no conceptual confusion here. But theologians have regularly wanted very much more from God's goodness than this, and it is hard to see how such a being as this could fit Galloway's description, "The God who is ethical Ground of the world guarantees the validity and persistence of the ethical values." [14]

Those who insist that God's goodness "passeth *all* understand-

---

[13] *Doctrine in the Church of England*, p. 40.
[14] Galloway, *The Philosophy of Religion*, p. 202.

ing" would feel that any definition or description would set limits to his goodness. When they speak of God's goodness, it is to say, "Praise Him! Praise Him!" But what is accomplished by such exhortation is far from clear.

There are other possible accounts of how God's goodness is necessary.

1. Some things can change and affect little else. God is not like that. God's goodness makes things not so bad as they might be. If God were to become evil, the result would be absolutely hellish. If one can both give meaning to and truly assert the hypothesis that God exists, then to conceive of God being otherwise than he is is no small matter, for it is to conceive of cosmic alterations in the way the world goes. That the law of gravity should cease to have application would have results of no greater generality. In this way we think of what is basic to the nature of the world as being more necessarily as it is than is something not so fundamental to the world.

2. Also, of course, there are countless reasons why men do evil that would not apply to God. For example, since God knows all, he cannot be victim (as can men) to unexpected temptation, nor can he lack insight into the nature of his actions. Self-deception, a real force for evil in men, would not be present in God. It is such nonself-contradictory and nonobscure facts about his nature that would give sense to the necessity of his goodness and that would really set him above his creatures. This is to make God a moral giant whose necessary goodness is different only in degree from that of men.

3. There is another account of the necessity of God's goodness that less obviously places the necessity elsewhere than in God's nature.

Prof. J. J. C. Smart gives an account of the necessity of God's existence that can be made to hold also for God's goodness.

# Perfect Goodness of God, II

Theological necessity cannot be logical necessity. In the second place, I think I can see roughly what sort of necessity theological necessity might be. Let me give an analogy from physics. It is not a *logical* necessity that the velocity of light in a vacuum should be constant. It would, however, upset physical theory considerably if we denied it. Similarly it is not a logical necessity that God exists. But it would clearly upset the structure of our religious attitudes in the most violent way if we denied it or even entertained the possibility of its falsehood.[15]

Mr. R. N. Smart makes what is in effect an application of this account in terms of the necessity of God's goodness.

Since the meaning of the expression "God" is largely determined by a fair number of statements in which it occurs (these being the more important doctrines of the theological system), it is not obvious that some of them may not be jettisoned without disqualifying us from using the expression in the other statements. Yet it could be objected that people would have a strong resistance to jettisoning the statement "God is good" without also abandoning the use of the expression elsewhere. . . . Expressions of wonder involve the ascription of sublimity and marvellousness to their target. In a monotheistic religion all this is concentrated upon the Creator of the world, to whom is thus ascribed what we may call supreme wonder-value. . . . The notion of sinfulness combines different inadequacies, the most important being moral culpability and God's wonder-value is expressed as the converse of sinfulness—as holiness, including goodness. Thus it becomes something like a theoretical requirement that God should be good. . . . Yet it is still sensible to deny this statement and without self-contradiction, *provided* it is recognized that the composite system would have to be sacrificed. Whether the

---

[15] A. G. N. Flew and A. MacIntyre, eds., *New Essays in Philosophical Theology* (London: S. C. M. Press, 1955), p. 40. Professor Smart no longer holds this position; cf. his "Philosophy and Religion," *Australasian Journal of Philosophy*, XXXVI (May, 1958).

system (including this requirement) is true or not depends above all on the evidence, and it is still open to us to choose another system or none at all. . . . The moral of all this is that the more deeply a requirement is written into a theological system, the more it looks like a definition. It becomes more heart-rending to allow an infringement; but this resistance does not lead to vacuity, because the requirement is related to the rest of the system, and the latter need not be vacuous. And a theoretical (or quasi-theoretical) impossibility is not a logical impossibility." [16]

According to this account, God is not *defined* as "the supreme wonder-value," but he is *described* in this way. Because, of course, if God were *defined* in this way it would follow that he was *defined* as "good," for "goodness" follows from "supreme wonder-value." Thus, the statement "God is good" would be true by logical necessity. Whether there was a being to whom the concept "God" could apply would be another matter. This would amount to the same thing as the view discussed in the previous section.

However, even if God is described, but not defined, in this way, God cannot be described as "supreme wonder-value" if he cannot also be described as "good." It is necessary—logically necessary—that if God is not good then he is not supreme wonder-value, for part of what is meant by "supreme wonder-value" is "good." If "God is good" is false then it follows by logical necessity that "God is the supreme wonder-value" is false. It does not follow that "God is the Creator of all things" is false. Perhaps this is what R. N. Smart means by a requirement being "written into a theological system." How many descriptions of a concept you can whittle away and still be said to employ the same concept is not always easy to say.

I think that it could not be denied that the notion of God is

---

[16] R. N. Smart, "The Perfect Good," *Australasian Journal of Philosophy*, XXXIII (Dec., 1955), 192–194.

defined in terms of what is allowable within the theological system. If there is some part of that system that is so essential that it cannot be scrapped without scrapping the whole system, then it would seem that that part is essential to the notion of God. This indeed "looks like a definition," and I am at a loss to see how it is not one.

But there is a kind of necessity involved in all of this that is not logical necessity. I might be unwilling to give up saying God was good because it would be upsetting or "heart-rending" to do so. It is somehow necessary for me to believe that a good God exists. If I gave up this belief, I should have to give up a whole way of life. This attitude is both repellent and attractive. I leave its further treatment to moralists and psychologists.

It is obvious that whatever sorts of necessity there may be in this account they do not apply to God or his nature. They apply either to the use of statements or the user of those statements. I believe that traditional theologians have wanted the necessity of God's goodness to be something about God.

In conclusion, there are three main accounts of God's goodness. One account is that in which the quality of unique and everlasting perfect goodness is made essential to the meaning instruction or naming instruction for the use of the term "God." Another account is that in which God is described as *in fact* good, so that he is some kind of moral giant of unimpeachable character but only better by far than we are and in his goodness not different in kind. Such a concept does not serve the theological requirements that God should be the Good and so the source of all goods. Another account is that in which God's goodness is described as entirely beyond human comprehension. Consistent with this account, there can be no rejoinder to someone's complaint that no meaning has been given to statements that purport to be about God and his goodness.

Those theologians to whom the argument of this chapter has

been directed are not of course left with nothing to say. In the face of our argument they will give not an answer but a mystery, and we are supposed to feel somehow, in some way, answered. They will tell us that our academic, philosophical puzzlings are resolved by the mystery of God's incarnation. There comes a time in the defense of the kind of theological assertions that we are considering when the claim is made that what is believed is beyond understanding. We shall examine in detail the nature of such a claim in a later chapter. Now let us try as best we can to speak clearly and leave what cannot be said for others to say.

As we have already seen, all seems to be well as long as the goodness of Christ is not really called in question. Theologians admit freely enough that if the goodness of Christ is in doubt then his divinity must be in doubt, and, of course, if the goodness of Christ is denied then it must also be denied that he is God. However, they think that there is nothing contradictory remaining if the goodness of Christ is asserted without qualification and he is called God, the Perfect Good. I have been at pains to point out that a contradiction of an irresoluble sort remains still. The contradiction is: Christ can be *conceived* to have been other (that is, not good) than he was, yet as God it should be not just false but *inconceivable* that he should have been not good.

Is the contradiction resolved by the theological device of the dual nature of Christ? Let the suggestion be that the human-finite nature of Christ is that which could have been otherwise and that the divine-infinite nature of Christ is that which could not have been otherwise. What is accomplished by this move?

We have assumed Christ's human nature to be good. This is supposed to allow for the consistent addition of the perfectly good divine nature. The divine nature cannot be asserted if the goodness of the human nature is called in question. But just what does this divine nature add?

It is that about Christ, when we assert his human nature to

be good, which could not have been otherwise. (Remember how Aquinas said that God being able to sin is "a contradiction in terms"; it is *inconceivable* that God should err, which is more than saying he never errs.) But *what* about Christ could not have been otherwise? *We can conceive to have been different from what it in fact was every individual thought, word, action, capacity, and disposition.* Let the divine nature express itself and by that expression contradict itself. Let the divine nature keep itself from all expression and by that sublime reticence say nothing to us. There is the choice between self-contradiction and vacuity.

# Five

# "Seeing" God

RELIGIOUS people may feel impatient with the harshness of argument in the last chapter. They may feel confident that they have something that nonreligious people lack, namely, a direct experience or apprehension of God. They may claim that such religious experience is a way of knowing God's existence. This claim must now be examined.

We shall first consider accounts of religious experience that seem to sacrifice an existential claim for the security of the feeling of the moment. There is an influential and subtle group of religious thinkers who would not insist upon any existential claim. My remarks are largely irrelevant to this group. It would be hasty to describe their religious belief as "subjective" or to employ any other such general descriptive term. For example, the "call," in even the most liberal and "subjective" Quaker sects, could not be reduced to statements about feelings. The "call," among other things, implies a mission or intricate pattern of behavior. The nonsubjective element of the "call" is evident,

## "Seeing" God

because insofar as one failed to live in accordance with a mission just so far would the genuineness of the "call" be questioned. It will be seen that this verification procedure is necessarily not available in the religious way of knowing to be examined.

In the second part of the chapter we shall consider accounts of religious experience that are not so easily reduced to mere subjectivity.

### I

We are rejecting logical argument of any kind as the first chapter of our theology or as representing the process by which God comes to be known. We are holding that our knowledge of God rests rather on the revelation of His personal Presence as Father, Son, and Holy Spirit. . . . Of such a Presence it must be true that to those who have never been confronted with it argument is useless, while to those who have it is superfluous.[1]

It is not as the result of an inference of any kind, whether explicit or implicit, whether laboriously excogitated or swiftly intuited, that the knowledge of God's reality comes to us. It comes rather through our direct, personal encounter with Him in the Person of Jesus Christ His Son our Lord.[2]

It will not be possible to describe the compelling touch of God otherwise than as the compelling touch of God. To anyone who has no such awareness of God, leading as it does to the typically religious attitudes of obeisance and worship, it will be quite impossible to indicate what is meant; one can only hope to evoke it, on the assumption that the capacity to become aware of God is part of normal human nature like the capacity to see light or to hear sound.[3]

---

[1] John Baillie, *Our Knowledge of God* (London: Oxford University Press, 1949), p. 132.

[2] *Ibid.*, p. 143.

[3] H. H. Farmer, *Towards Belief in God* (London: S. C. M. Press, 1942), Pt. II, p. 40.

## Religious Belief

The arguments of the theologians quoted have been taken out of context. The quotations by themselves do not give a faithful or complete impression of their total argument. The following quotations from Professor Farmer indicate two further lines of argument which cannot be discussed here.

For what we have now in mind is no demonstrative proofs *from* the world, but rather confirmatory considerations which present themselves to us when we bring belief in God with us *to* the world. It is a matter of the coherence of the belief with other facts. If we find that the religious intuition which has arisen from other sources provides the mind with a thought in terms of which much else can without forcing be construed, then that is an intellectual satisfaction, and a legitimate confirmation of belief, which it would be absurd to despise.[4]

We shall first speak in general terms of what may be called the human situation and need, and thereafter we shall try to show how belief in God, as particularized in its Christian form (though still broadly set forth), fits on to this situation and need.[5]

The alleged theological way of knowing may be described as follows: I have direct experience (knowledge, acquaintance, apprehension) of God; therefore I have valid reason to believe that God exists. By this it may be meant that the statement "I have had direct experience of God, but God does not exist" is contradictory. If so, the assertion that "I have had direct experience of God" commits one to the assertion that God exists. From this it follows that "I have had direct experience of God" is more than a psychological statement, because it claims more than the fact that I have certain experiences—it claims that God exists. On this interpretation the argument is deductively valid. The assertion "I have direct experience of God" includes the assertion "God exists." Thus, the conclusion "Therefore, God exists" follows tautologically.

---

[4] *Ibid.*, p. 113.   [5] *Ibid.*, p. 62.

Unfortunately, this deduction is useless. If the deduction were to be useful, the addition of the existential claim "God exists" to the psychological claim of having religious experiences would have to be shown to be warrantable, and this cannot be done.

Consider the following propositions: (1) I feel as if an unseen person were interested in (willed) my welfare. (2) I feel an elation quite unlike any I have ever felt before. (3) I have feelings of guilt and shame at my sinfulness. (4) I feel as if I were committed to bending all my efforts to living in a certain way. These propositions state only that I have certain complex feelings and experiences. Nothing else follows deductively. The only thing that I can establish beyond possible correction on the basis of having certain feelings and experiences is that I have these feelings and sensations. No matter how unique people may think their experience to be, it cannot do the impossible.

Neither is the addition of the existential claim "God exists" to the psychological claim made good by any inductive argument. There are no tests agreed upon to establish genuine experience of God and distinguish it decisively from the nongenuine.[6] Indeed, many theologians deny the possibility of any such test or set of tests.

The believer may persuade us that something extraordinary has happened by saying, "I am a changed man since 6:37 P.M., May 6, 1939." This is a straightforward empirical statement. We can test it by noticing whether or not he has given up his bad habits. We may allow the truth of the statement even if he has not given up his bad habits, because we may find evidence of bad conscience, self-searchings and remorse that had not been present before that date.

However, if the believer says, "I had a direct experience of God at 6:37 P.M., May 6, 1939," this is not an empirical statement in the way that the other statement is. How could we check its

---

[6] This will be qualified in the second part of this chapter.

truth? No matter how much or how little his subsequent behavior, such as giving up bad habits and so on, is affected, it could never prove or disprove his statement.

An important point to note is that theologians tend to discourage any detailed description of the required experience ("apprehension of God").[7] The more naturalistic and detailed the description of the required experience becomes, the easier would it become to deny the existential claim. One could say, "Yes, I had those very experiences, but they certainly did not convince me of God's existence." The only sure defense here would be for the theologian to make the claim analytic: "You couldn't have those experiences and at the same time sincerely deny God's existence."

The way in which many theologians talk would seem to show that they think of knowing God as something requiring a kind of sixth sense. The Divine Light is not of a color usually visible only to eagles, and the Voice of God is not of a pitch usually audible only to dogs. No matter how much more keen our senses became, we should be no better off than before. The sixth sense, therefore, must be very different from the other five.

This supposed religious sense has no vocabulary of its own but depends upon metaphors drawn from the other senses. There are no terms which apply to it and it alone. There is a vocabulary for what is sensed but not for the sense. We "see" the Holy, the Numinous, the Divine. In a similar way we often speak of "hearing" the voice of conscience and "seeing" logical connections. By using this metaphor we emphasize the fact that often we come to understand the point of an argument or problem in logic suddenly. We mark this occurrence by such phrases as "the light dawned," "understood it in a flash." Such events are usually described in terms of a complete assurance that one's interpreta-

---

[7] The detailed descriptions of the Catholic mystics will be discussed later.

tion is correct and a confidence that one will tend to be able to reproduce or recognize the argument or problem in various contexts in the future. But a vitally important distinction between this "seeing" and the religious "seeing" is that there is a checking procedure for the former but not for the latter. If, while doing a problem in geometry you "see" that one angle is equal to another and then on checking over your proof find that they are not equal after all, you say "I didn't really 'see,' I only thought I did."

The religious way of knowing is described as being unique. No one can deny the existence of feelings and experiences which the believer calls "religious," and no one can deny their power. Because of this and because the way of knowing by direct experience is neither inductive nor deductive, theologians have tried to give this way of knowing a special status. One way of doing this is to claim that religious experience is unique and incommunicable.

Professor Baillie, in likening our knowledge of God to our knowledge of other minds, says that it is "like our knowledge of tridimensional space and all other primary modes of knowledge, something that cannot be imagined by one who does not already possess it, since it cannot be described to him in terms of anything else than itself." [8] This kind of comparison is stated in the two sentences following, and we shall now examine the similarities and dissimilarities between them. (1) You don't know what the experience of God is until you have had it. (2) You don't know what the color blue is until you have seen it. Farmer says, "All the basic elements in our experience are incommunicable. Who could describe light and colour to one who has known nothing but darkness?" [9] All that Farmer proves is that a description of one group of sensations A in terms of another set of

---

[8] Baillie, *Our Knowledge of God*, p. 217.
[9] Farmer, *Towards Belief in God*, p. 41.

69

sensations B is never sufficient for knowing group A. According to this definition of "know," in order to know one must have those sensations. Thus, all that is proved is that, in order to know what religious experience is, one must have a religious experience. This helps in no way at all to prove that such experience is direct apprehension of God and helps in no way to support the existential claim "God exists."

Farmer makes the point that describing the experience of God to an unbeliever is like describing color to a man blind from birth. So it is, in the sense that the believer has usually had experiences which the unbeliever has not. However, it is also very much unlike. The analogy breaks down at some vital points.

The blind man may have genuine, though incomplete knowledge of color. He may have an instrument for detecting wave lengths, and the like. Indeed, he may even increase our knowledge of color. More important still, the blind man may realize the differences in powers of prediction between himself and the man of normal eyesight. He is well aware of the fact that, unlike himself, the man of normal eyesight does not have to wait to hear the rush of the bull in order to be warned.

This point concerning differences in powers of prediction is connected with the problem of how we are to know when someone has the direct experience of God or even when we ourselves have the direct experience of God. It was shown above how the situation is easier in the case of the blind man knowing about color. It is only when one comes to such a case as knowing God that the society of tests and checkup procedures, which surround other instances of knowing, completely vanishes. What is put in the place of these tests and checking procedures is an immediacy of knowledge that is supposed to carry its own guarantee. This feature will be examined later.

It is true that the man of normal vision has a way of knowing color which the blind man does not have, that is, he can see colored objects. However, as we have seen, it would be wrong to insist that this is the only way of knowing color and that the blind man has *no* way of knowing color. Perhaps Farmer has this in mind when he tries to make an analogy between the incommunicability of the believer's direct knowledge of God to the unbeliever and the incommunicability of the normal man's knowledge of color to the blind man. The analogy is justified if "knowing color" is made synonymous with "having color sensations." On this account, no matter how good his hearing, reliable his color-detecting instruments, and so on, the blind man could not know color, and the man of normal vision could not communicate to him just what this knowledge would be like.

The believer has had certain unusual experiences, which, presumably, the unbeliever has not had. If "having direct experience of God" is made synonymous with "having certain religious experiences," and the believer has had these and the unbeliever has not, then we may say that the believer's knowledge is incommunicable to the unbeliever in that it has already been legislated that in order to know what the direct experience of God is one must have had certain religious experiences. "To anyone who has no such awareness of God, leading as it does to the typically religious attitudes of obeisance and worship, it will be quite impossible to indicate what is meant; one can only hope to evoke it." [10] Reading theological textbooks and watching the behavior of believers is not sufficient.

The theologian has made the analogy above hold at the cost of endangering the existential claim about God which he hoped to establish. If "knowing color" is made synonymous with "having color sensations" and "having direct experience of God" is made synonymous with "having certain religious experiences," then it is certainly true that a blind man cannot "know color" and that a nonreligious man cannot "have direct experience of

---

[10] *Ibid.,* p. 40.

God." By definition, also, it is true that the blind man and the nonreligious man cannot know the meaning of the phrases "knowing color" and "having direct experience of God," because it has been previously legislated that one cannot know their meaning without having the relevant experiences.

If this analogy is kept, the phrases "knowing color" and "having direct experience of God" seem to make no claim beyond the psychological claims about one's color sensations and religious feelings.

If this analogy is not kept, there is no sense in the comparison of the incommunicability between the man of normal vision and the blind man with the incommunicability between the believer and the unbeliever.

If "knowing color" is to be shaken loose from its purely psychological implications and made to have an existential reference concerning features of the world, then a whole society of tests and checkup procedures, which would be wholly irrelevant to the support of the psychological claim about one's own color sensations, become relevant. For example, what other people see, the existence of light waves, and the description of their characteristics, which needs the testimony of research workers and scientific instruments, all must be taken into account.

Because "having direct experience of God" does not admit the relevance of a society of tests and checking procedures, it tends to place itself in the company of the other ways of knowing which preserve their self-sufficiency, "uniqueness," and "incommunicability" by making a psychological and not an existential claim. For example, "I seem to see a piece of blue paper," [11] requires no further test or checking procedure in order to be considered true. Indeed, if Jones says, "I seem to see a piece of blue paper," he not only needs no further corroboration but cannot be shown to have been mistaken. If Smith says to Jones, "It

---

[11] I shall call such statements "low-claim assertions."

does not seem to me as if I were seeing a piece of blue paper,"
this cannot rightly raise any doubts in Jones's mind, though it
may express Smith's doubts. That is, Smith may feel that Jones
is lying. However, if Jones had said, "I see a piece of blue paper,"
and Smith, in the same place and at the same time, had replied,
"I do not see a piece of blue paper," or, "It does not seem to me
as if I were now seeing a piece of blue paper," then Smith's remarks can rightly raise doubts in Jones's mind. Further investigation will then be proper, and if no piece of paper can be felt
and other investigators cannot see or feel the paper and photographs reveal nothing, then Jones's statement will be shown to
have been false. Jones's only refuge will be to say, "Well, I certainly seem to see a piece of blue paper." This is a perfect refuge,
because no one can prove him wrong, but its unassailability has
been bought at the price of making no claim about the world
beyond the claim about his own experience of the moment.

The closeness of the religious statement to the psychological
statement can be brought out in another way, as follows. When
one wishes to support the assertion that a certain physical object
exists, the tests and checking procedures made by Jones himself
are not the only things relevant to the truth of his assertion.
Testimony of what others see, hear, and so on is also relevant.
That is, if Jones wanted to know whether it was really a star
that he saw, he could not only take photographs, look through a
telescope, and the like but also ask others if they saw the star. If a
large proportion of a large number of people denied seeing the
star, Jones's claim about the star's existence would be weakened.
Of course, he might still trust his telescope. However, let us now
imagine that Jones does not make use of the tests and checking
procedures (photographs and telescopes) but is left with the
testimony of what he sees and the testimony of others concerning what they see. In this case, it is so much to the point if a
large number of people deny seeing the star that Jones will be

considered irrational or mad if he goes on asserting its existence. His only irrefutable position is to reduce his physical object claim to an announcement concerning his own sensations. Then the testimony of men and angels cannot disturb his certitude These sensations of the moment he knows directly and immediately, and the indirect and nonimmediate testimony of men and angels is irrelevant. Absolute confidence and absolute indifference to the majority judgment is bought at the price of reducing the existential to the nonexistential.

The religious claim is similar to, though not identical with, the case above in certain important features. We have seen that there are no tests or checking procedures open to the believer to support his existential claim about God. Thus, he is left with the testimony of his own experience and the similar testimony of the experience of others. And, of course, he is not left wanting for such testimony, for religious communities seem to serve just this sort of function.

Let us imagine a case comparable to the one concerning the existence of a physical object. In this case Brown is a professor of divinity, and he believes that he has come to know of the existence of God through direct experience of God. In order to understand the intricate character of what Professor Brown is asserting we must imagine a highly unusual situation. The other members of the faculty and the members of Professor Brown's religious community suddenly begin sincerely to deny his, and what has been their own, assertion. Perhaps they still attend church services and pray as often as they used to do, and perhaps they claim to have the same sort of experiences as they had when they were believers, but they refuse to accept the conclusion that God exists. Whether they give a Freudian explanation or some other explanation or no explanation of their experiences, they are agreed in refusing to accept the existential claim (about God) made by Professor Brown. How does this affect Professor

Brown and his claim? It may affect Professor Brown very deeply —indeed, he may die of broken-hearted disappointment at the loss of his fellow believers. However, the loss of fellow believers may not weaken his confidence in the truth of his assertion or in the testimony of his experience. In this matter his experience may be all that ultimately counts for him in establishing his confidence in the truth of his claim about the existence of God. It has been said that religious experience carries its own guarantee, and perhaps the account above describes what is meant by this.

It is quite obvious from these examples that the religious statement "I have direct experience of God" is of a different status from the physical object statement "I see a star" and shows a distressing similarity to the low-claim assertion "I seem to see a star." The bulk of this chapter has so far been devoted to showing some of the many forms this similarity takes. Does this mean then that the religious statement and its existential claim concerning God amount to no more than a reference to the complex feelings and experiences of the believer?

Perhaps the best way to answer this question is to take a typical low-claim assertion and see if there is anything which must be said of it and all other low-claim assertions which cannot be said of the religious statement. One way of differentiating a physical object statement from a low-claim assertion is by means of prefixing the phrase "I seem." [12] For instance, the statement "I see a star" may be transformed into a statement concerning my sensations by translating it into the form "I seem to see a star." The first statement involves a claim about the existence of an object as well as an announcement concerning my sensations and there-

---

[12] This, clearly, is a superficial and mechanical move, for the prefixing of this phrase ordinarily would result in a qualified and hedging physical object statement. I shall just have to plead that the possibility that such a prefixing should result in a low-claim assertion is here realized.

fore subjects itself to the risk of being wrong concerning that further claim. Whether one is wrong in this case is determined by a society of tests and checking procedures such as taking photographs and looking through telescopes and by the testimony of others that they see or do not see a star. The second statement involves no claim about the existence of an object and so requires no such tests and no testimony of others; indeed, the final judge of the truth of the statement is the person making it. If no existential claim is lost by the addition of this phrase to a statement then the assertion is low-claim. For instance, the statement "I feel pain" loses nothing by the addition "I seem to feel pain."

In the case of the religious statement "I have direct experience of God" the addition of the phrase is fatal to all that the believer wants to assert. "I seem to be having direct experience of God" is a statement concerning my feelings and sensations of the moment, and as such it makes no claim about the existence of God. Thus, the original statement "I have direct experience of God" is not a low-claim assertion. This should not surprise us. We should have known it all along, for is it not an assertion that ones comes to know something, namely God, by means of one's feelings and sensations and this something is not reducible to them? The statement is not a low-claim one just because it is used to assert the existence of something. Whether this assertion is warranted and what exactly it amounts to is quite another question.

We are tempted to think that the religious statement must be of one sort or another. The truth is that *per impossible* it is both at once. The theologian must use it in both ways, and which way he is to emphasize at a particular time depends upon the circumstances of its use and most particularly the direction of our probings.

The statement "I seem to be having direct experience of God" is an eccentric one. It is eccentric not only because introspective announcements are unusual and because statements about God have a peculiar obscurity but for a further and more important reason. This eccentricity may be brought out by comparing this statement with others having the same form. A first formulation of this may be put in the following way. In reference to things other than our sensations of the moment knowledge is prior to seeming as if.

The statement "I seem to be looking directly at a chair" has a meaning only insofar as I already *know* what it is like to look directly at a chair. The statement "I seem to be listening to a choir," has a meaning only insofar as I already *know* what it is like to be listening to a choir. The assumption of knowledge in both these cases is one which all normal people are expected to be able to make and do in fact make.

The statement "I seem to be having direct experience of God" does not lend itself so easily to the criterion for meaning exemplified above, because if this statement has meaning only insofar as one already *knows* what it is like to have direct experience of God, the assumption of such knowledge is certainly not one which all normal people may be expected to be able to make or do in fact make. However, it may be said that the assumption of such knowledge as knowledge of what it is like to see a gorgon may not be made of all normal people and, therefore, the case of religious knowledge is in no peculiar position. This objection can be answered when we ask the question "How do we come to learn what it would be like to look directly at a chair, hear a choir, see a gorgon, have direct experience of God?"

It is not that there are no answers to the question concerning how we come to learn what it would be like to have direct experience of God. We are not left completely in the dark. Instead, the point is that the answers to this question are quite different from the answers to the questions concerning how we come to learn what it would be like to look directly at a chair, hear a choir, and see a gorgon. No one in our society has seen a gorgon, yet there are people who, by means of their specialized knowledge of mythical literature, may claim in a perfectly meaningful way that it now seems to them as if they were seeing a gorgon.

Let us imagine a society in which there are no chairs and no one knows anything at all about chairs. If we were to try to teach one of the members of this society what it would be like to see a chair and if we were not allowed to construct a chair, what might we do? We might look around at the furniture and say, "A chair is a kind of narrow settee. It is used to sit on." This would be a beginning. Then we might compare different settees as to which are more chairlike. We might draw pictures of chairs, make gestures with our hands showing the general shape and size of different sorts of chairs. If, on the following day, the person being instructed said, "I had a most unusual dream last night—I seemed to be looking directly at a chair," we should admit that his statement was closer in meaning to a similar one which we who have seen chairs might make than it would be to a similar one which another member might make who had no information or instruction or experience of chairs. We would insist that we had better knowledge of what it is to see a chair than has the instructed member of society who has still actually to see a chair. However, to know pictures of chairs is to know about chairs in a legitimate sense.

But let us now imagine a utopian society in which none of the members has ever been in the least sad or unhappy. If we were to try to teach one of the members of this society what it would be like to feel sad, how would we go about it? It can be said that giving definitions, no matter how ingenious, would be no help; drawing pictures of unhappy faces, no matter how well drawn, would be no help, so long as these measures failed to evoke a feeling of sadness in this person. Comparing the emotion of sadness with other emotions would be no help, because no matter how like other emotions (weariness and the like) are to sadness they fail just because they are not sadness. No, sadness is unique and incomparable.

To anyone who has no such awareness of sadness, leading, as it does, to the typically unhappy behavior of tears and drawn faces, it will be quite impossible to indicate what is meant. One can only hope to evoke it on the assumption that the capacity to become aware of sadness is part of normal human nature like the capacity to see light or to hear sound.

This last paragraph is a play upon a quotation given at the very beginning of this chapter. The following is the original version.

To anyone who has no such awareness of God, leading as it does to the typically religious attitudes of obeisance and worship, it will be quite impossible to indicate what is meant; one can only hope to evoke it, on the assumption that the capacity to become aware of God is part of normal human nature like the capacity to see light or to hear sound.[13]

Consider the following statements:

1. We are rejecting logical argument of any kind as the first chapter of our epistemology of aesthetics, or as representing the process by which beauty comes to be known.

2. It is not as the result of an inference of any kind, whether explicit or implicit, whether laboriously excogitated or swiftly intuited, that the knowledge of beauty comes to us.

3. To those who have never been confronted with the experience of seeing the beauty of something, argument is useless.

As these statements stand, they are plainly false. Professors of aesthetics and professional art critics often do help us to come to

---

[13] Farmer, *Towards Belief in God.* p. 40.

"knowledge of beauty" by all kinds of inference and arguments. They may, and often do, help us to come to a finer appreciation of beautiful things. Knowledge of the rules of perspective and understanding of an artist's departure from them is relevant to an aesthetic appreciation of his work.

However, it is possible to interpret these statements as true, and this is more important for our purpose. There is sense in saying that an art critic, who has vastly increased our aesthetic sensitivity and whose books of art criticism are the very best, may never have known beauty. If there are no signs of this critic ever having been stirred by any work of art, then no matter how subtle his analyses, there is sense in claiming that he has never been confronted with the experience of seeing the beauty of something. This sense just is that we may be determined not to say that a person has seen the beauty of something or has knowledge of beauty if he does not at some time have certain complex emotions and feelings which are typically associated with looking at paintings, hearing music, and reading poetry. To "know beauty" or to "see the beauty of something" here means, among other things, to have certain sorts of emotions and feelings.

The statements on aesthetics given above are a play on a quotation given at the beginning of this chapter. The following is the original version with the appropriate omissions and transpositions.

We are rejecting logical argument of any kind as the first chapter of our theology or as representing the process by which God comes to be known. . . .

It is not as the result of an inference of any kind, whether explicit or implicit, whether laboriously excogitated or swiftly intuited, that the knowledge of God's reality comes to us.

. . . To those who have never been confronted with it [direct, personal encounter with God] argument is useless.[14]

———
[14] Baillie, *Our Knowledge of God*, pp. 132, 143.

As these statements stand they are plainly false. Professors of divinity and clergymen are expected to do what Baillie claims cannot be done.

However, it is possible to interpret these statements as true, and this is more important for our purpose. There is sense in saying that a theologian (who has vastly increased our religious sensitivity and whose books of theology are the very best) may never have known God. If there are no signs of this theologian's ever having been stirred by a religious ritual or act of worship, then, no matter how subtle his analyses, there is sense in claiming that he has never been confronted with God's personal Presence. This sense just is that we are determined not to say that a person has knowledge of God if he does not at some time have certain complex emotions and feelings which are associated with attending religious services, praying, and reading the Bible. To "know God" or to be confronted with God's "personal Presence" means, of necessity, having certain sorts of emotions and feelings.

In this section the analogy between seeing blue and experiencing God has been examined and found to be misleading. I shall not deal in this chapter with the connexion between what the believer expects from immortality and his religious belief. This peculiar kind of test or verification has special difficulties which will be treated in another chapter.

So far I have tried to indicate how statements concerning a certain alleged religious way of knowing betray a logic extraordinarily like that of statements concerning introspective and subjective ways of knowing. It is not my wish to go from a correct suggestion that the logic is *very, very* like to an incorrect suggestion that their logic is *just* like that of introspective and subjective statements, for, after all, such statements are logically in order.

I have argued that one cannot read off the existence of God

from the existence of religious experience. Now, I must insist, in all charity, that *neither* can one read off the *non*-existence of God from the existence of religious experience.

In criticizing some of the foregoing argument, Mr. W. D. Glasgow claims,

> It is essential here for the defender of the religious way of knowing to assert that there are cases where a man *knows* himself to be experiencing an objective Deity, just as there are cases where he knows himself to be experiencing a subjective pain. Unless it is insisted that there is such a thing as *cognitive experience* in religion, Martin's assimilation of all religious existential statements to psychological statements (or what ought to be called psychological statements) becomes highly plausible. Indeed, even the phrase "*may* be objective" has no meaning, probably, for Martin, unless theoretically at least it is possible to find out or test whether religious experience *is* objective. The position is only saved, again, if we say that in some cases the agent himself anyhow *does* know.[15]

Glasgow cannot mean "a man *knows* himself to be experiencing an objective Deity" *in just the same way as* "he knows himself to be experiencing a subjective pain." One's pain is not a thing that exists independently of one's experience. I do not establish the existence of my pain on the basis of experience. There is nothing to establish beyond the experience. Presumably there is something to establish on the basis of religious experience, namely, the presence of God. When Glasgow says "there is such a thing as *cognitive experience* in religion" and "in some cases the agent himself anyhow *does* know," he must be read as saying that the presence of God is known on the basis of religious experience. That is, the presence of God is something over and above the

---

[15] W. D. Glasgow, "Knowledge of God," *Philosophy*, XXXII (1957), 236. This article is a criticism of my article "A Religious Way of Knowing," printed in Flew and MacIntyre, *New Essays in Philosophical Theology* (London: S. C. M. Press, 1955), pp. 76–95.

experience itself. The model that Glasgow implies is that a cognitive experience is rather like a photograph of a friend: one can read off from the photograph that it is of that friend: and though this is a misleading model, there is something in it. If I am sitting at my desk and someone asks me if there is an ash tray on my desk, *all* that I have to do is have a look and say "Yes" or "No." But whether or not I know there is an ash tray on my desk is not to be read off simply from what my eyes at that moment told me. For if my eyes can tell me the truth they can tell me a lie, and the difference here would not be decided by what they tell. For me really to have seen and known there was an ash tray, other people must have been able to have seen it if they had looked. If I have only the testimony of my eyes and discount all else, then that testimony is mute concerning the existence of what is external. My eyes can tell me (in an hallucination) of the presence of an ash tray when there is no ash tray.

When someone uses the sentence "I see an ash tray" in such a way that he counts as relevant to its truth *only* his visual experience at the time, he is talking *only* about that experience, though the sentence has the form of making a statement about an ash tray. It does not help if he calls it a "cognitive experience" or if he says that he "anyhow *does* know" or if he says that his experience is "self-authenticating" or is a "direct encounter." We cannot allow a speaker any final authority in the account of how he is using his sentences. If such special dispensation were allowable, conceptual confusion would be rare indeed.

Similarly, I have argued, when someone uses the sentence "I have or have had direct experience of God" in such a way that he counts as relevant to its truth *only* his experience at the time, he is talking *only* about that experience, though the sentence has the form of making a statement about the presence of God, and neither does it help if he calls it a "cognitive experience."

## Religious Belief

From the fact that someone uses the sentence "I see an ash tray" so that he is talking *only* about his visual experience, nothing at all follows about whether or not he is actually seeing an ash tray in front of him. His *statement* may be only about his visual experience itself, and his actual *situation* may be that of seeing the ash tray. Also, from the fact that someone uses the sentence "I have or have had direct experience of God" in such a way that he is talking *only* about his experience at the time, nothing at all follows about whether or not he is actually experiencing the presence of a supernatural being. His *statement* may be only about his experience itself, and his actual *situation* may be that of experiencing the presence of a supernatural being.

The religious person will want, in what he says, to be able to distinguish between a "delusive" and a "veridical" experience of God. The experience should be due to the actual presence of God and not due only to a drug or to self-deception or to the action of Satan. Therefore he must use his sentence to refer to more than an experience that is, in principle, compatible with these and other similar causes.

What makes a form of experience a way of knowing? It is often suggested that the mystic who "sees" God is like a man (in a society of blind men) who sees colors. It is claimed that each has a form of experience and a way of knowing that others lack. Let us now work out this analogy. A society of blind men is told by one of its members that he has come to have a form of experience and a way of knowing by means of which he has been able to discover the existence of things not discoverable by ordinary experience. He says that these things have a *kind* of size (not just like size as it is felt by the blind) and a *kind* of shape (not just like shape as it is felt by the blind); he further says that these things are somehow "everywhere" and that they cannot expect to understand what these things are like and what he means by experiencing them unless they themselves have these experiences. He then tells them of a procedure by which they will be able to discover for themselves the existence of these things. He warns them that these things do not always reveal themselves when the procedure is carried out, but, if a person is sufficiently diligent and believes strongly enough in their existence, he will probably come to know by means of unique and incomparable experiences of the existence of these things.

Some people, with faith and diligence, submit themselves to the required procedure, and some of these are rewarded by a kind of experience they have not known before. Color shapes float before them—things that they cannot touch or feel and that are beyond the reach of their senses, and things that may be present to one of their group and not experienced by the others, things that may as well be everywhere as anywhere, since they are locatable only in the sense of being "before" each observer to whom they appear. These people cannot correlate this new form of experience with the rest of experience, they cannot touch or smell these "things." Indeed, they "see" visions, not things. Or rather these people have no way of *knowing* the existence of the things that may or may not exist over and above the momentary experiences. May these experiences all the same be "cognitive"? Yes and no. Yes, there may be something, they know not what, responsible for their having these experiences. No, their experiences are not a way of *knowing* about this something. For the experience of a colored shape that needs no corroboration by the experience of others similarly placed, and that is not related to one's other senses, is not in itself a way of knowing what in the world is responsible for this experience even if there is something beyond the condition of the "observer" that is so responsible. So far, even the people concerned have no *way of knowing* what more is involved than the fact of their experiencing momentary "visions."

## Religious Belief

I have not denied that the religious mystic may have experiences that others do not. Neither have I denied that there might be some external agency responsible for these experiences. What I have denied is that the mystic's possession of these experiences is in itself a way of knowing the existence or nature of such an agency.

The argument of this chapter lies in an area in which confusion is common. I shall consider two cases of such confusion especially relevant to what I have been saying.

You are acquainted with the distinction between feeling and emotion. Feeling, such as pleasure or pain, is in itself a purely subjective experience; emotion implies an objective situation within which there is something which arouses the emotion, and towards which the emotion is directed. The Divine is, it would seem, first experienced in such a situation; and is initially apprehended solely and exclusively as that which arouses certain types of emotion. If the emotion be awe, then the Divine is so far apprehended as the awesome, what Otto has so helpfully entitled the numinous.[16]

There are two questionable assumptions here: first, that whether or not an experience refers to an objective state of affairs can be read off from the experience itself; second, that emotions *must* do so.

The second claim that an emotion as such implies an objective situation can be refuted very simply. My feeling of pleasure while watching a game of football is related to something in my environment, but my feeling of pleasure at a tune running through my head is not. My emotion of awe in the presence of a particularly magnificent race horse is related to something in my environment, but my emotion of awe during a dream of a coronation service is not. Some people have aesthetic emotions

---

[16] N. Kemp Smith, *Is Divine Existence Credible?*, British Academy Lecture (London: British Academy, 1931), p. 23.

aroused by the contemplation of mathematical proofs and theorems, and others have the emotion of fear toward ghosts and goblins.

In a criticism of the argument of the first part of this chapter (as originally published in "A Religious Way of Knowing," in *Mind,* October, 1952) Professor H. D. Lewis seems to be making the first claim, that a reference to an objective state of affairs can be read off from the experience itself.

He [Martin] seems to think that the only claim to objectivity which an experience may have is that which is established by tests and checking procedures. A man's statement that he "seems to see a blue piece of paper" is thus said to be unassailable only because it is a "claim about his own state of mind." This I would doubt, for the colour expanse which we only seem to see is neither a mere appearance nor a state of mind. It is "out there before me" and real enough while I seem to see it, however many problems may be involved in distinguishing between it and physical entities. . . . "Having been stirred" by a religious ritual or act of worship, or having "certain sorts of emotions and feelings," is not the essential thing in religious experience; it is what we apprehend that comes first.[17]

However, "what we apprehend," if anything, is the whole problem and cannot "come first." Certainly, people have had special sorts of experience which incline them to claim with the greatest confidence that their experiences are of God. But whether the experiences are or are not of God is not to be decided by describing or having those experiences. For whether anything or nothing is apprehended by experiences is not to be read off from the experiences themselves. The presence of a piece of blue paper is not to be read off from my experience as of a piece of blue paper. Other things are relevant: What would a photograph reveal?

---

[17] H. D. Lewis, "Philosophical Surveys X, The Philosophy of Religion, 1945–1952," *Philosophical Quarterly,* IV (July, 1954), p. 263.

Can I touch it? What do others see? It is only when I admit the
relevance of such checking procedures that I can lay claim to
apprehending the paper, and, indeed, the admission of the
relevance of such procedures is what gives meaning to the assertion that I am apprehending the paper. *What I apprehend is the
sort of thing that can be photographed, touched, and seen by
others.*

It does not help when Lewis says,

The colour expanse which we only seem to see is neither a mere
appearance nor a state of mind. It is "out there before me" and
real enough while I seem to see it, however many problems may
be involved in distinguishing between it and physical entities.

Think now of a man who claims to see a blue piece of paper, and
when we complain that we cannot, he replies, "Oh, it isn't the
sort of thing that can be photographed, touched, or seen by
others, but all the same, it is out there before me." Are we to
think that he has come upon a special sort of object that is nevertheless "out there" as are desks and tables and the rest of the
furniture of the world? No, ontological reference is something to
be earned. We earn the designation "out there" of a thing by
allowing its presence to be determined by the procedures we all
know. We cannot just *say* "out there" of it, and we cannot just
*say* "apprehended" of God.

It can be objected, "But God is different, and we never meant
that our experiences of God should be checked by procedures
relevant to physical objects." Of course not, but what *sort* of
checks are there then, so that we are left with more than the
mere experiences whose existence even the atheist need not
deny?

## II

Yet checking procedures are not on all accounts in all ways
irrelevant. As in all theological discourse concerning the status of

religious experience there are many, many voices, and so far we have listened to too few.

A religious experience is not just an ineffable, indescribable something that comes and goes unbidden and amenable to no criteria of identity. At least, the mystics seldom describe it in this way. There are certain steps one can take to bring about such experiences, and the experiences are describable within limits, and they leave certain kinds of identifiable aftereffects.

Alvarez de Paz and other mystics have emphasized the importance of practicing austerities, conquering the flesh, and mortifying the body.

Of course, this training of the body is not sufficient. The mind must be trained as well. To have a vision of the Holy Virgin one must be acquainted with the basic facts of "Christ's birth and life and death." To have the highest mystical apprehension of the Trinity, as did St. Teresa, one must have some elementary theological training.

Nor is bodily and intellectual training enough, for there must be moral and emotional training as well. The commandment to love one another was given not only to lead us to peace and brotherhood on earth but also to change our hearts so that we might see God.

Yet all of these may not be enough, for it is possible one should train oneself most assiduously in all of these ways and still not have truly religious experience. This possibility is characterized by saying that finally the favor and grace of God are required.

The paradoxical and negative ways in which mystics most often describe their experiences may seem, at first, unsatisfactory. But it helps to consider how similar sorts of descriptions are employed outside the religious context. One might say of one's emotion at a particular time that one felt both love and hate toward someone. This would be understood as a description of a complex emotion that most of us have experienced. And the paradoxical expression is not reducible to "in some ways love, in other ways hate," because it refers not only to different patterns of behaving and feeling but also to a particular feeling at a particular moment.

Alvarez de Paz gives a particularly sharp description that must strike even the most sceptical reader as in no way obscure or evasive.

One perceives no representation of the face or the body, yet one knows with greater certainty than if one saw it with one's eyes that the person (Jesus Christ or the Blessed Virgin) is present on one's right hand or in one's heart. . . . It is as if, in darkness, one should feel at once that someone is at one's side, knowing that he has goodwill and not enmity towards you; while one remains absolutely ignorant whether it is a man or a woman, young or old, handsome or ugly, standing or seated.[18]

It would be wrong for us to legislate against the mystic's claim that his experience is not sensory. For in a nonreligious context there may be a parallel. Many of us have felt or experienced the presence of some loved one dead or living but distant. (Of course, we do not tend to think that the person is in any way *actually* present unless the person is dead.) Certainly in such cases we do not see or hear the person. It is not even *as if* we heard or saw the person. Making the parallel even closer to the mystical, we do not even have to have any kind of mental image of the loved one. Neither is the presence felt as being in any specific place. The very subtle feelings and emotions typically directed to this one person and no other are now aroused as once they were by this person alone. The unique love and regard this person showed us, we, as it were, receive again. And we can feel ashamed at having done things of which the loved one would

---

[18] Quoted in Joseph Marechal, *Studies in the Psychology of the Mystics* (London: Burns Oates & Washbourne, 1927), p. 110.

disapprove. And so we can feel guided where there is no guide and loved where the lover is dead. The emotion is in shadow felt but is no less real for that.

A child may read of a fairy-story giant who eats the children who do not think he is real and even some who do. He is described in detail (perhaps there is even a picture), and his hatred of children is made too clear. The child may have a bad dream about the giant. Or he may, as in the case above, just feel the giant's presence in no very localized place yet somewhere near. That is, the child reads the story, comes to feel a kind of fear toward the giant, and hates him in a way that others do not. Then the child, hearing and seeing nothing, may, in the dark, feel that fear and sense that hate so strongly that he will claim, even when the light is turned on and in spite of the most tender parental reassurance, that the giant had been in the room. That is, the experience of the child is such that he is left with a certitude which he considers the giant alone could give.

In order to have such an experience, then, will all of the sense of reality and conviction that it carries, it is not necessary that the being whose presence is so felt should ever have existed.

As children we are taught to love Christ in a very special way, and we are taught of Christ's very special love for us. Christ, as a person, is made extremely real to us. That we cannot see or hear him takes very little from his reality. He was once seen and heard, and we are told so much of his life and actions and visible love that we are apt to feel that we know him more clearly than we do any other historical person. As children (or, indeed, as adults) we are encouraged in this feeling by being told that he is somehow, if not actually somewhere, alive. We are told that God loves us as Christ loves us, and we learn that Christ and God are somehow One. So we know roughly how we *should* feel in God's presence. We have as reference countless stories of how others have felt. These experiences are very different, but they form a kind of family. At one extreme there is a visible vision, and at the other extreme there is almost a kind of unconscious trance.

Let us now speak of the sign which proves the prayer of union to have been genuine. As you have seen, God then deprives the soul of all its senses that he may the better imprint in it true wisdom; it neither sees, hears, nor understands anything while this state lasts. . . . God visits the soul in a manner which prevents its doubting, on returning to itself, that it dwelt in him and that he was within it. . . . But, you may ask, how can a person who is incapable of sight and hearing see or know these things? I do not say that she saw it at the time, but that she perceives it clearly afterwards, not by any vision but by a certitude which remains in the heart which God alone could give. . . . If we did not see it, how can we feel so sure of it? That I do not know: it is the work of the Almighty and I am certain that what I say is the fact. I maintain that a soul which does not feel this assurance has not been united to God entirely, but only by one of its powers, or has received one of the many other favours God is accustomed to bestow on men.[19]

Yet, with all of this, it could be argued that all that has been accomplished is a description of a class of experiences and of methods of obtaining and recognizing them. Their ontological reference has still to be established. It could be dogmatically asserted that these experiences by definition come only through the grace of God, but this would be no more than a way of stamping one's foot and insisting on, rather than arguing for, that reference. St. Teresa once again is of help. She was plagued during her lifetime not by doubts about the character of her experiences but about their source. Was she perhaps being subtly deceived by

---

[19] St. Teresa, *Interior Castle* (London: Thomas Baker, 1930), pp. 91–93.

Satan? She was not at a loss to provide a kind of settlement procedure.

I could not believe that Satan, if he wished to deceive me, could have recourse to means so adverse to his purpose as this, of rooting out my faults and implanting virtues and spiritual strength: for I saw clearly that I had become another person by means of these visions. . . . Neither the imagination nor the evil one could represent what leaves such peace, calm, and good fruits in the soul, and particularly the following three graces of a very high order. The first of these is a perception of the greatness of God, which becomes clearer to us as we witness more of it. Secondly, we gain self-knowledge and humility as we see how creatures so base as ourselves in comparison with the Creator of such wonders, have dared to offend Him in the past or venture to gaze on Him now. The third grace is a contempt of all earthly things unless they are consecrated to the service of so great a God.[20]

But now, what more has really been accomplished by this? To say that the source of these experiences is God and not Satan in the absence of further criteria reduces to saying that these experiences have certain sorts of profound effects upon one's character, attitudes, and behavior. And why should an atheist deny any of this? If there is more that cannot be so reduced and if it is inconsistent with the claims of an atheist, it still remains to be said.

Unlike the first section of this chapter, this section has been concerned with views (those of the great Catholic mystics) in which statements about religious experience are not employed as in any way arguments for, or evidence of, the existence of God. The mystics are convinced on other grounds of the existence of God. Religious experience, then, is conceived by them as a way of coming to know better the object of their worship, whose ex-

---

[20] *Ibid.*, p. 171.

istence is proved or assumed independent of that experience.

This conservative estimate of the status of religious experience in theology is not, however, necessarily safe from censure. The conceptual weight is shifted from the experience to the previously established or assumed notion of the object of the experience. In the previous chapter difficulties were found in typical notions of the qualities of God. No Catholic theologian and few Protestant theologians would claim that religious experience could resolve problems of this conceptual sort.

# Six

# Life after Death

PEOPLE sometimes look forward to life after death as a means of settling questions concerning the existence and nature of God. In so doing they make three assumptions, each of which could be called into question. It has been contended by some atheists that the very notion of personal survival of death is logically incoherent. Theists who look to the life to come must therefore establish, in the first place, that survival is at least conceivable. Secondly, they must show that it actually takes place, and, thirdly, they must show that survival, if it takes place, proves the existence of God. In this chapter the first and the third of these assumptions will be examined.

Is it conceivable that a person should survive death? Can we understand what this would be like? Certainly we can imagine something surviving. What we have to be sure of, however, is that what we imagine as surviving is the very same person as the person that died. What we must look into first of all, therefore, is the question of what it is that makes the man John Smith identical with the boy of years ago, and more generally what does personal identity consist in? It seems as though there must be some chain that binds together the person of today with the very same person tomorrow. But what is this chain? Is it the body? Is the person continuous only if the body is continuous? Or must there be an exact resemblance or continuity between the soul at one time and the soul at another?

This can be treated by means of three cases.[1]

1. Some people have spoken as if the chain of identity were the body. This is not so. Imagine that I stand before a mirror and see the familiar countenance change into that of a terrible hairy beast. It does not matter whether this happens suddenly or gradually or if there is a disappearance of the body for a time in between. The person who changed into an enormous beetle in the Kafka story "Metamorphosis" suffered most horribly from this bodily change, but he retained his memory, hopes, loves, and sensitivity, and the change was not that of one person into another, though it most certainly was a change from one kind of body into another.

If Merlin were to tell me that he was going to make me disappear (*totally* without trace and without transporting me to another place) for five minutes and then make me appear again, I think that I should be worried. I would have fears that that might be the end of me, that Merlin might fail to do the latter half of the trick. Yet if bodily continuity were the chain of personal identity, Merlin's suggestion should be nonsense. If bodily continuity is necessary, then it would be self-contradictory to assert that Merlin could make me appear again. All he could do would be to make someone exactly like me appear. That, I think, would be good enough for me. It is important to see that it is merely a matter of convention what we say here. Most of us would say

---

[1] Reference must be made to Anthony Flew's admirable article, "Locke and the Problem of Personal Identity," *Philosophy*, XXVI (Jan., 1951).

that Merlin could bring the same person back, and, if he kept on doing the trick, we would all say this, if only because it is a more economical way of stating the fact. It is a strange case, and it is philosophical dogma to claim that we must describe it in only one way.

Something of the same sort can even be said of physical objects. Suppose Merlin presented me with a pearl of great beauty. Taking note of his smile when giving it to me, I wait for the unexpected. Of one thing I am sure, it is no ordinary pearl. Yes, at either regular or irregular intervals it disappears and re-appears. Or *must* there be a different pearl each time? I see no necessity here. So even for physical objects, spatiotemporal continuity can break down. Or if you choose to say the object is different with each appearance, do not say it *must* be, for here it is just a matter of what you choose to say. The shocking and hard-to-accept thing is that there is such a large element of verbal legislation and linguistic convention concerning the identity of people and physical objects.

The body, then, as the chain of the soul is not necessary, so perhaps the chain is that of memory and the capacities of mind and heart. And, who knows more of these capacities than the man himself?

2. Imagine that A is sleeping on a bed, and, still asleep, arises and stands in the middle of the room. At the moment of his waking, two people B and C *exactly* like A just appear out of thin air, and A does not see them appear but on waking finds them standing there seeming to be waking. After the confusion has died down, it turns out that these two seem to remember the same things (even the same dream) and to have the same capacities as A. They, in every way, exactly resemble one another. How do they decide the question which of them is the real A? There is nothing about their seeming to remember or their capacities of heart and mind that would reveal this to them. There

is no procedure open to them, and there is no procedure open to others. But there *could* be. If there had been other observers in the room, watching closely, then they could tell which were the persons who just appeared and which was the person who was there all along. No "state of consciousness" or anything of the inner spirit could reveal this to A, B, or C.

Now, it may be objected, "True, in some cases the body is the chain of identity and in others the inner life is the chain of identity. It can still be said that one or the other *must* be present, as a sign or criterion of sameness of soul."

This suggests that there *must* be something about a person that marks him as the same as the person he seems to remember himself to be. It may not be the seeming to remember in itself that ensures identity, but after all either A has the memory or not, and so either A is identical with the person he remembers himself to be or not. Something must *make* the memory a memory and guarantee self-identity, and it must be present in the person or soul now. Our very language suggests this. Our hope of life after death insists upon it.

The stage is now set for our third case.

3. Once again, A is sleeping on a couch. Observers are in the room and see that he vanishes in thin air. They are driven closer to the brink of madness a few moments later by the appearance out of thin air of B and C. These two individuals, it turns out, are absolutely like A in body, in the ways outward and inward in which they seem to remember, and capacities, and propensities of mind and heart. I do not ask, "What would we say?" for heaven knows what we would say. In discussions of self-identity, philosophers capitalize on certain features of our language and assert that something must always be the case, and our present series of cases is designed to refute this and to disturb a model inherent in our language. The purpose should not be to legislate concerning what we would or should say. The purpose and im-

portance of the case is that there is *nothing,* absolutely *nothing,* in the way of criteria by means of which B and C, or others, can decide which one has the memory of doing what A did. If it did not seem to rule out the frantic situation of A's wife, I should say that the question "Which is the *real* A?" had no sense.

Let us now consider a parallel case concerning physical objects.

A number of people are looking at couch A and see suddenly a bookcase in its place or see it gradually transform itself into an ink bottle. To say that couch A is "in" the bookcase or ink bottle would be a perverse way of remarking upon how the bookcase or ink bottle are historically connected with couch A. But history and spatiotemporal continuity are not sufficient even for the identity of physical objects. There is little temptation to insist that couch A and the bookcase or ink bottle are really the same thing. There is no inner life that can remain the same.

Observers looking at couch A in the corner see couches B and C appear out of thin air. They are in every way identical with A. The couches are not concerned to identify themselves with what they seem to remember. The observers have no difficulty in identifying A.

In another case observers see couch A disappear in thin air and several moments later couches B and C appear out of thin air. There is no temptation for us to assert that one of them *must* be A and that there *must* be a way of telling.

Couches and people are different. In the crucial third case, B and C seem to remember themselves as A. This brings up the question of memory, but the nature of the case makes it pointless. In the parallel case of couches B and C there is nothing to force the question upon us, and its pointlessness shows itself. Our model of the soul and the chain of self-identity suggests that the question of memory can *never* be pointless. (It is perhaps less misleading to say that this is a place where you can say what you like rather than a place to say "pointless.")

99

## Religious Belief

Mr. B. A. O. Williams in an article "Personal Identity and Individuation" [2] treats very differently cases similar to some of those that have just been considered.

Williams introduces what has become almost a stock kind of puzzle case. It is the case of a man, Charles, who after sleeping, wakes seeming to remember witnessing "certain events and doing certain actions which earlier he did not claim to remember" and who under questioning "could not remember witnessing other events and doing other actions which earlier he did remember." These witnessings of events and doings of actions are part of the life history of one and only one person—Guy Fawkes.

If it is logically possible that Charles should undergo the changes described then it is logically possible that some other man should simultaneously undergo the same changes; e.g. that both Charles and his brother Robert should be found in this condition. What should we say in that case? They cannot both be Guy Fawkes; if they were, Guy Fawkes would be in two places at once, which is absurd. Moreover if they were both identical with Guy Fawkes, they would be identical with each other, which is also absurd. Hence we could not say that they were both identical with Guy Fawkes. We might instead say that one of them was identical with Guy Fawkes, and that the other was just like him; but this would be an utterly vacuous manoeuvre, since there would be *ex hypothesi* no principle determining which description was to apply to which. So it would be best, if anything, to say that both had mysteriously become like Guy Fawkes, clairvoyantly knew about him, or something like this. If this would be the best description of each of the two, why would it not be the best description of Charles if Charles were changed?

Williams goes on to say that, because "we could not speak of identity" in the case of Charles and Robert, this does not prove

[2] *Aristotelian Society Proceedings*, LVIII (1957). The passage quoted is on pages 238–239.

that we "cannot speak of identity" in the case of Charles alone. Then he goes on, "Certainly it is no proof. Yet the argument does indicate that to speak of identity in the simpler case would be at least quite vacuous."

It is hard to see the force of Williams' argument that Charles and Robert "cannot both be Guy Fawkes; if they were, Guy Fawkes would be in two places at once, which is absurd. Moreover, if they were both identical with Guy Fawkes, they would be identical with each other, which is also absurd." This argument cannot possibly hold against the assertion that Guy Fawkes has become Charles and Robert or the assertion that Charles and Robert have in the past had an identical life history. This is evident if we consider the case of an amoeba that divides into two.[3] The original amoeba has become two, and these two have in the past had an identical life history, that is, when they were one. We understand perfectly well how what has become two is able to be in two places at once and how, though the two divisions are not identical with each other, they are identical with the original undivided amoeba.[4] That is, a full life history of any one of the two amoebae would include reference to the original amoeba in a way in which the full life history of two other exactly similar amoebae would not. The criterion of identity that Williams is anxious to defend, bodily continuity, is applicable (whether we

---

[3] It might be said that each of the two amoebae is identical with parts of the original amoeba. I do not think that this is an objection to anything I say.

[4] It is true that we do not ordinarily say that the divided amoebae are identical with the original amoeba. This is because amoebae are not concerned with identifying themselves, and we are not concerned with identifying them. It is not important to us. Even so, one scientist might ask another to observe an amoeba through the microscope, and the second scientist might look and say, "But there are two amoebae," to which the first scientist could reply, "They must be the same one divided into two."

apply it or not) right back to the original amoeba.[5] On the basis of Williams' argument we should be forced to say that the two amoebae are merely exactly similar to and in *no way* to be identified with the original amoeba. Yet this would be false.

Unfortunately, Williams has not made enough of a puzzle of his case. As he describes it, I think even the newspapers may agree with his conclusion, though this does not correct the invalidity of his arguments. A more seductive case can be devised.

Let us suppose that person A completely disappears without trace, vanishes into thin air, passes out of existence.[6] Persons B and C appear out of thin air. They exactly resemble A in every possible way; they have similar bodies; they seem to remember doing what A alone did; and so on. A more forceful argument in defense of Williams' thesis may be introduced. It may be said that the case of Charles and Robert (or better still, B and C) and the case of the amoebae are different. The difference between "The two amoebae are merely exactly similar to the original" and "The original became two" is established by means of bodily continuity. The difference between "B and C are merely exactly similar to A" and "A became B and C" cannot be established by means of bodily continuity, because A completely disappeared and is supposed to have passed out of existence. Therefore, to say that B and C are the same as A is just to say

---

[5] The amoeba is in this way different from the mother and child. At any stage in the reproductive process the child can be set beside the mother. This is why we do not think of the case as one in which what was one (mother) has become two (mother and child).

[6] To say "pass out of existence" is to say more than "disappear without trace," yet I do not see how it is necessarily an irrational thing to say. It may be as well to point out that, for anyone who holds strictly to the spatiotemporal continuity criterion for identity, *it will be as impossible to say that something disappears from one place and appears in another place without any journeying as it will be to say that something ceases to exist and then begins to exist again.*

that they are exactly similar to A. This argument is very nearly right, but it is misleadingly put.

Those who make bodily continuity essential to identity stress that, if in the case of B and C we say they are the same as A (that is, that A has become two), we are cutting the use of "same" loose from the criterion of bodily continuity and therefore changing its sense. This is true. But they go too far when they say that here the sense of "same" just comes to the sense of "exactly similar." For they act as if, as a description of this peculiar case, "exactly similar" had undergone no change of sense. But it has. We must look more closely at this phrase.

1) "Exactly similar" may be used so as to be utterly neutral to the problem of identity. It may just describe bodily and mental characteristics. One might say, "I don't know whether that chap over there is the same as the fellow we met last night or not but they are exactly similar." One also might say, "Alfred in 1951 is exactly similar to Alfred in 1956." In this case "exactly similar" does not rule out "same."

2) "Exactly similar" may also be used in *contrast* to "same." It would then be used in the same way as the less ambiguous phrase "merely exactly similar." Bert in 1956 may be exactly similar to Alfred in 1951, and we may say of him, "Exactly similar to Alfred in 1951," as a way of distinguishing him from Alfred. This sense is at home in those situations in which the contrast with "same" or "identical" is straightforward. We say, "This pearl is exactly similar to the one you had yesterday." We mean that it is not the same and that it could be placed side by side with the other if that other could be found or had not dissolved in acid. We mean also that their life history is not connected.

Let us return to the case of Merlin's pearl. *Must* it be a different, though exactly similar, pearl each time? I see no necessity here. Surely another question is of great relevance. If the pearl that Merlin gave me had not disappeared, would I now hold a host of pearls that came from nowhere? If A had not disappeared, would B and C have appeared? In this second sense "exactly similar" carries with it the notion of actual or possible comparison (putting side by side) at the same time. It is this feature that marks "exactly similar" off from "same" or "identical." It is not possible to put a thing side by side with itself (the same or identical thing). We cannot in *this way* compare Alfred in 1951 with himself in 1951 or 1956.

If we are to compare something X in 1956 with something else Y in 1951, we must allow that Y has or *might have* continued to exist until 1956 without changing any of the features that we consider important so that Y could be set beside X. If Y had ceased to exist in 1952 and if we suppose that contrary to fact Y had continued to exist and that X would still have existed in 1956,[7] then it follows that X and Y are not the same or identical, though they may be exactly similar.

The case of Merlin's pearl and the case of B and C may now be judged. Are we to say that the pearl that appears is the same as the original pearl or that the disappearance of the original is causally related to the appearance of another pearl exactly similar to the first?[8] Are we to say that B and C are the same as A, that is, that they are A become two,[9] or are we to say that the

---

[7] This account assumes a certain analysis of counterfactuals. This is not the place to give such an analysis, though I think it is of the first importance to do so. I believe that a counterfactual can be true against the balance of relevant evidence or where there is no evidence whatever.

[8] I do not mean these alternatives to be exhaustive. They are the important ones for my purposes.

[9] It seems to me just prejudice to insist that B or C and not both can be in any way identified with A. The insistence upon the emptiness of trying to choose between B and C as to which is really A has *point* only if it has been established that *only* one can in any way be identified with A.

disappearance of A is causally related to the appearance of two different things B and C exactly similar to A? Whatever we say, it is essential to see that the sense of "same" and the sense of "exactly similar" have both undergone a change when applied to these peculiar cases. Ordinarily "same" carries with it as criterion something of bodily continuity. It does not do so when applied to these cases.

Ordinarily "exactly similar" carries with it as a criterion actual or possible comparison (putting side by side) at the same time. It does not do so when applied to these cases. If someone were to ask me what should be said here, "same" or "merely exactly similar," I think that I should tell him to flip his own coin. This sounds and is a little too cavalier. It overemphasizes the element of conventionality. After all, there could be reason for adopting one convention rather than another. If it often happened that when something disappeared something *very* different appeared, we would probably say that one thing's appearance was caused by the other's disappearance instead of saying that the same thing appeared again. If this sort of happening were a regular feature of the world, and if on one occasion something disappeared and something exactly like it appeared, we would probably still say that one thing's appearance was caused by the other's disappearance instead of saying that the same thing appeared again. However, if it regularly happened that things disappeared and exactly similar things appeared, it would be an almost unavoidable economy to speak of them as the same.

It is such considerations as this that would incline us to adopt one convention rather than another. It is not easy to accept the fact that there is such an element of verbal legislation and linguistic convention concerning the identity of people and physical objects when their situation is described in terms of the puzzle cases. We are inclined to think that our ordinary concepts of "same" and "different but exactly similar" must be ready-made for application to any situation. This is not so. They do, however, serve us admirably well in the world as it is.

The master tautology which lies as the foundation of the chain of identity is "I am the same person that I was and I will be the same as I am." This sentence could be used in such a way that it would be necessarily false. That is, by growing older we change and are now not what we were, if only that we are older. It could also be used to be just false. Some people never change, are always the same, but most of us do. It can also be used so that the use of "I" and "same person" makes it self-contradictory to deny. Then it is a tautology and has a wonderful, but barren, security.

When we say "I," we want it to point to something and not be able to fail. It points in the present without fail, without danger of contradiction, but nowhere else—not to the past and not to the future. "I did X and I am doing Y" is a statement from which it follows analytically that "the same person did X and is doing Y." But "I did X" can be denied without contradiction not only because I did not in fact do X but more importantly on the grounds that the person who is doing Y did not exist at the time of X. This is not of real concern to us in our daily lives. (People are not born into the world or suddenly appear who seem to have the most certain memories of having done things on earth before they came into being.) It comes to be of real concern when we think of death and the sudden exit of people from this world and wonder about the sudden appearance of people into the next. We want some certain means of ensuring that the people who leave this world and who enter the next are the same. I have tried to show that the certainty we desire is not a possible one. It is when our ordinary criteria for decision as to whether it is the same person are broken down (as in death) that we cry out for some really ultimate criterion that could not fail. I want to be *sure* that someone in the next life will have a memory of having himself done what I have done in this life. There *must* be a something that is continuous and identical in this life that will survive into the next. I have tried to show how this insistence is ultimately pointless, and if the notion of personal survival rests upon this insistence then it is also pointless.[10]

Difficulties concerning the personal identity of disembodied spirits are even more acute. We shall soon question whether the notion of a disembodied spirit is meaningful, but first let us consider a simple case that reveals the oddity of identifying such spirits. John and Henry are brothers who know a great deal about one another's past. Something unfortunate happens: John gets the idea he is Henry, and Henry gets the idea he is John. John seems to remember doing what Henry did, and Henry seems to remember doing what John did. They are put away for treatment. Later a friend asks, "Is John all right now?" and if John has come out of his delusion under the treatment we can answer, "Yes." But now suppose John and Henry die before the treatment has had any effect and a friend asks, "I wonder if John is all right now?" If John and Henry are disembodied spirits what possible criteria for their identity could be appealed to in order to answer the nightmare question? Yet divine judgment demands an answer.

The problem of disembodied existence after death is of practical as well as of theoretical interest. It is a difficult as well as an important problem, and I must confess that I have no great confidence in the adequacy of the arguments that I shall raise concerning this issue.

The question "Can men live on after death without their bodies?" is like a request to people empty places. These colorless shades that cast no shadow and stir no curtain intrude without

---

[10] Someone might object, "You just casually forget that Christ rose from the dead and promised us that we should do the same and that we should see God." It is not clear that we whose bodies shall be turned to dust are in the same position as Christ.

notice the privacy of my most private place. They may live by multitudes under my clothing or under my skin. How many angels on the head of a pin? How many souls inhabit my limbs? And just what kind of nonsense is this if nonsense it be?

At first sight the question "Can I, myself, survive death without a body?" seems easily settled in the affirmative by the simple means of a slight feat of the imagination. Surely I can imagine the following scene. I am lying on my deathbed with the members of my family gathered around me. My breathing becomes more difficult until I can breathe no more. The doctor closes my eyes, and still I see his face and hear the weeping. Without effort or resistance I find myself moving above the bed and now, owning no body, I view the body that was my own.

What I can imagine to be true of myself must be conceivable of others. How then can there be any serious confusion in the notion of disembodied existence when I seem to be able to imagine this disembodied state so easily? The imagination *can* play conceptual tricks. People sometimes dream or think that they can imagine with ease themselves to have *really* been someone else and not just *like* someone else. This is to imagine nonsense. Therefore, I see no prima-facie objection to arguing, as I shall attempt to do, that what might at first be thought to be clearly imaginable is really a confusion.

It is tempting to think that our perceptions of the physical world are made up of two aspects: the mental sensory experience and the physical object to which the experience corresponds. The physical conditions of observation, including the state of the perceiver's body, are considered to be merely *causally* necessary for the sensory experience to occur as it does. Those features of the situation in which the physicist has interest, such as the passage of light rays from the object to the retina, and those features of the situation in which the physiologist has interest, such as the condition and reaction of the retina and brain, are features that are merely causally necessary for the perception to take place, and these causal features are therefore logically dispensable.

The picture of perception suggested by this account is that of two essential aspects, namely, the visual reaction (that is, the looking to an observer to be an object of a certain kind) and the actual presence of an object of that kind plus the inessential or logically, if not factually, dispensable aspect of the causal trappings in the situation. This picture is a distortion. We can see that this is so if we consider the following case. Someone is sitting looking at a patch of light. An expert physiologist knows that if he inserts a very fine needle into a particular area of the person's brain that person will have a visual response exactly similar to his visual response to the patch of light. While the subject is still looking at the patch of light, the physiologist inserts the needle and at this moment the subject closes his eyes. The subject notices no difference, the visual reaction is the same as it was, and the patch of light is still before him on the wall. Does he still *see* the patch of light? Surely not, because now the existence and nature of the patch has *nothing* to do with his visual reaction. Indeed, it might as well be no longer before him.

What a thing is depends upon how it reacts to and reacts upon other things. A thing that can exist quite apart from the existence of sentient beings is *partly* to be described in terms of how a sentient being under certain physical conditions will have certain visual, tactual, and similar reactions in its presence. This is the picture of perception, in very rough outline, that I want to substitute for the one that I have just criticized. It is this criticized view of perception that lends itself to the effortless supposition of disembodied existence.

There are some who would argue that it makes no sense to speak of disembodied spirits perceiving, but who would not wish to argue that the notion of disembodied existence has no sense. Mr. Peter Geach says,

Even an earthworm, though, affords some handholds for the application of "sensuous" psychological concepts; we connect its writhings when injured with our own pain-reactions. But when it comes to an automaton, or again if we are invited to apply the concepts to a supposed disembodied existence, then we may be sure that we are right in refusing to play; too many threads are broken, and the conceptual web has collapsed.[11]

The argument seems to be that we have public, behavioral criteria for the application of " 'sensuous' psychological concepts" like seeing, hearing, feeling afraid, feeling hungry, and having a pain, and where the behavioral criteria do not apply the concepts lose sense. But Geach goes on to say,

Denying sense to the attempt to think of feelings, sensations, emotions, etc., apart from a living organism may seem to be practically the same as denying disembodied mind altogether. Such a denial does not follow, nor has it historically always been held to follow. Aquinas, for example, believed that there were wholly disembodied intelligences: . . . the evil spirits in hell are tormented not by aches but by the frustration of their wicked will. . . . Sensuous experiences are possible only in connexion with a living organism. . . . The old problem was rather: "How can a being that thinks and judges and decides *also* have sensuous experiences?" It was "intellectual" acts like judgment, not just *anything* that would now be called "consciousness," which seemed to Aquinas to be wholly incommensurable with events in the physical world; for him, the "unbridgeable gulf" was at a different place.[12]

It is difficult to see how Geach's argument can be made consistent. If he is right in saying that the "sensuous" psychological

---

[11] P. T. Geach, *Mental Acts* (London: Routledge and Kegan Paul, 1957), pp. 114–115.
[12] *Ibid.*, pp. 116–117.

concepts require public, behavioral criteria for their meaningful application, the same will hold true of the "intellectual" psychological concepts. We learn whether someone is in pain, feels afraid or sees an object before him, by noting what he does and what he says. Otherwise, we cannot speak of pain, fear, and seeing. Similarly, it would seem that we learn about someone's thoughts, judgments, and decisions by noting what he does and what he says. Otherwise, we cannot speak of thinking, judging, and deciding. True, a man can keep his thoughts to himself, as he can also keep his fears and pains to himself.

The argument might be replaced by the claim that the "sensuous" feelings, sensations, and emotions are locatable in the body, whereas the "intellectual" thoughts, judgments, and decisions are not. But are visual impressions in the head behind the eyes? Certainly no more so than is the thought when we do a calculation in our heads. The ultimate sense of locating a visual impression or emotion is location with the observable person who has them. They are locatable as happening to *him*. Thoughts, judgments, and decisions, if they are anything, we locate with the observable person, who by his inner speech or overt action thinks, judges, and decides. They are locatable in terms of *his* covert and overt activity.

If both "sensuous" and "intellectual" psychological activities and processes are locatable primarily in terms of the individual, the individual cannot then be "located" or identified by them. And, of course, he is not. The individual person is a separable, identifiable, observable organism. But, now, if his "sensuous" and "intellectual" psychological activities are to be identified and located by identifying and locating *him*, how is *he* to be identified and located in a disembodied state?

Yet, in the teeth of argument, we may be unmoved, for we may still feel that no argument can prove to be unthinkable that which we can so easily imagine. At least, concerning *myself*, I can imagine that I should be disembodied. If arguments suggest otherwise, they are invalid. This looks like the end of argument, but I think that it is not.

When I describe for myself my disembodied state, is this describing my mental life without a body? Not necessarily. There are many things that I can describe, without having to mention anything else, that cannot exist by themselves. I can describe a thing's shape without having to mention its size. From this it does not follow that I have described or can describe a thing that has shape but no size. Similarly, I can describe my mental life without mentioning anything about my body. It does not follow that I have described or can describe my mental life existing without a body.

When I have a visual image or think something to myself, I do not have to locate the person who has the image or thought. Indeed, there could be no procedure for my doing so. I do not have to succeed in picking myself out from my environment in order to be able to say "I," as I have to succeed in picking someone else out from his environment in order to be able to say "He." For I cannot fail to indicate one and only one person when I say "I," but I can fail to indicate one and only one person when I say "He," because the person I indicate may be a figment of my imagination. Yet the person indicated when I say aloud or to myself "I" must be an individual that is separable from his physical and social environment, and, when others succeed in picking me out from this environment by seeing and hearing me, I must have indicated the object they observe when I said "I." But if the individual I indicated when I said to myself "I" can exist disembodied, what does that individual have to do with the object actually observed by others?

The question "Can experiences and intellectual processes exist without a body?" can be reformulated "Can one formulate a statement that is *only* about an experience or intellectual process?"

At first, the answer seems obviously "Yes." The statement "I am in pain" or the statement "I shall think about survival" seem to be clear examples. But each statement makes reference to an individual who is in pain and who has decided to think about a problem. The pain experience and the decision have been ascribed to something that might not have been in pain and might not have made that decision, and that might not have been at that time in any way conscious, though not for that reason nonexistent. I do not know how to ascribe an experience to an individual that cannot be thought to have been able to exist without any experience at that time.

The attempt to get at experiences in the raw or rather to formulate statements that are only about experiences might seem to succeed by the simple device of dropping the personal pronoun. "Similarly, 'I have (had) frightful pain' really says no more than 'That pain is (was) frightful'; the question *whose* pain it is does not arise if the remark is a soliloquy."[13] But one can soliloquize or talk to oneself about the pain of another. The form of words "That pain is (was) frightful," might in a soliloquy be a statement about oneself or about someone else. Which it is depends upon whether the words are used to make the statement "I am (was) in frightful pain" or the statement "He is (was) in frightful pain." I conclude that there is no way of making a statement about an experience *only* without making reference to the individual having that experience, who at that time might have had a different experience or no experience at all.

Someone who thinks that he can think of himself as just a series of experiences may try to say that to ascribe an experience to a disembodied spirit is to "place" that experience as a member

---

[13] *Ibid.*, p. 120.

of a series of experiences. And he may claim that to say that an experience is ascribed to an individual who at that time might have had a different experience or no experience is simply to say that that series of experiences might, at the time, have had a different member or no member at all. I think that this defense will not work.

If disembodied spirits are series of experiences, if experiences are occurrences of a certain duration, and if experiences are to be understood only by being ascribed to individuals who at that time might not have had any experience, then it follows that a single (qualitatively similar and continuous) experience cannot occur. For an unchanging pain of a certain duration that is not a member of a series of experiences, but occurs by itself, cannot be ascribed to any individual, since one has lost *all* reference to that which might not have had any experience at the time. So the ascription of one experience only to an individual would be devoid of sense. From this it would follow that the existence of a particular experience logically entails the existence of other experiences serially related to it. I do not see how this entailment can hold. I do not see how the existence of a particular thing entails that other things should exist as well.

Someone might claim, in the face of all of the argument above that a single experience just *could* occur without any need of an individual having the experience, and further maintain that the supposition that there was such an individual merely amounted to the supposition that this experience was serially related to other experiences. The trouble with this conceptual scheme is that it can provide no conceivable principle of individuation for the numerical differentiation between a number of qualitatively similar single experiences existing at the same time. It will be seen that placing the experiences as members of one or more series of experiences does not help.

# Life after Death

Several further difficulties provide logical embarrassment for those who believe in the possibility of disembodied existence.

1. Usually it is said that experiences are those things that are privately had by individuals. It is not supposed to make sense to say that a particular experience could have been had by someone other than the individual who had it or that a particular experience could be had by more than one person. This is expressed by the slogan, "Only I can have my pain." That is, if someone else feels a pain, it must in virtue of being felt by a different person be numerically, if not qualitatively, different from mine. Thus, the statement "Only I can have my pain" is different from the statement "Only I can have my money." Unlike my pain, my money can be shared and could conceivably have been owned by another. Yet, on the supposition that a disembodied spirit is a series of experiences, it would seem to be just a matter of fact that an experience was a member of one series and not another. If this is a matter of fact, what was in fact a member of one series might conceivably have been a member of another series.

2. If several disembodied spirits have qualitatively similar experiences at the same time, it would seem possible that there should be just one experience which is a common member of several distinct series. This would be for the different series to interlock. How then can this possibility be differentiated from the possibility that there should be several exactly similar, but numerically different, experiences? What point is there in making numerical differentiation at all between qualitatively similar experiences occurring at the same time?

3. Furthermore, if a particular experience is a member of one series for a certain duration and then immediately afterwards a qualitatively similar experience is a member of another series, what difference is there between saying that there are two numerically distinct experiences and saying that there is one

experience that begins as a member of one series and at a later stage of its duration is a member of another series?

4. Finally, if the experiences of disembodied spirits are all qualitatively similar, how can we distinguish logically between the case of there being one and only one series of experiences and the case of there being more than one series of experiences? It will be no argument to say that the series are differentiated from one another by their connection with different series of experiences in past embodied states, for we have seen that there is no logical reason for denying the possibility that a particular experience should be a common member of many different series, and so there will be no logical reason for denying the possibility of many different series of experiences in embodied states being related to a future disembodied *single* series of experiences. Therefore, there can be no principle of individuation between one such series and more than one series of experiences. An afterlife of qualitatively similar experiences may as well be said to be solipsistic as pluralistic.

The difficulty is not overcome by the suggestion that the experiences of disembodied spirits are not qualitatively similar, for there still would be no way of differentiating between a single series of experiences and a multitude having qualitatively similar experiences, and a multitude of disembodied series of experiences may as well be serially related to a single past embodied series as may a single disembodied series. Consistent with the thesis of disembodied existence there seems no way of giving point to the identity or numerical distinctness of experiences. Until this is done, I cannot give sense to the notion of disembodied existence itself.

The suggestion that the concept "soul" may be employed to provide a principle of individuation requires that this concept be given content. I do not see any way of doing this.

The relevance of survival to knowledge of God must now be

discussed. "For now we see through a glass, darkly; but then face to face: now I know in part; but then shall I know even as also I am known" (I Cor. 13:12).

The model that is involved in the notion that we shall have knowledge of God by means of a kind of introduction in the next life could not be more obvious. A veil is to be lifted, a door opened, and we shall see what is now hidden. But the model is a bad one. For our lack is not a "face to face" encounter with God. Our lack is that with God we do not know what it would be to lift the veil. If we have *no* idea of what it would be like to find a thing, we then have given no meaning to saying it is hidden. Herein lies the difficulty and obscurity of theological statements, because the theologian will object that it is not true that he has no idea of what it would be like to find God after death. He smiles when we speak of looking and listening for God in the next life, and his smile broadens as we remark that we will and could be no better off then than now for this sort of thing. He says, "You are determined to take what I say literally, when I speak analogically. If you will only listen, you are told by the Bible and religious thinkers something of what to expect from the next life and how it is related to the existence of God and our knowledge or acquaintance with God."

How do we come to know of God in this world? "The heavens declare the glory of God; and the firmament showeth his handiwork" (Psalms 19:1). "By night an atheist half believes a God" (*Night Thoughts*, Edward Young). There are things in the world that speak of God and other things that speak as clearly of Satan. It is important to bring this up here, because the signs of God and Satan are promised to be clearer in the next world. (I shall assume for argument that the supposition of an afterlife is a meaningful one.) Piety and goodness is to have its reward and impiety and evil its punishment. Reward and punishment is to be meted out with perfect mercy and justice, and the judgment is to be forever. There will be no hiding. There are times now when all of us must feel like creatures in the grip of a higher power. For some of us this speaks of God. In the next life this feeling is to be inescapable and universal. Now, perhaps we know why the theologian smiled and why the smile chafed against us. Behind it was the threat: "You just wait. It is not a question of your finding God, He will find *you*."

And they shall be my people, and I will be their God:

And I will give them one heart, and one way, that they may fear me for ever, for the good of them, and of their children after them:

And I will make an everlasting covenant with them, . . . to do them good; but I will put my fear in their hearts, that they shall not depart from me. [Jer. 32:38-40]

And the kings of the earth, and the great men, and the rich men, and the chief captains, and the mighty men, and every bondman, and every free man, hid themselves in the dens and in the rocks of the mountains;

And said to the mountains and rocks, Fall on us, and hide us from the face of him that sitteth on the throne, and from the wrath of the Lamb:

For the great day of his wrath is come; and who shall be able to stand? [Rev. 6:15-17]

We may be tempted to retort, "All right, all right, so nice things will happen to nice people and bad things to bad people, and all people will be a little mad, because they will have this feeling of a controlling higher power. People will still be no better off and *could* be no better off than we are for *really* finding God. You continually use analogies without saying where they hold." This objection has some force, but it is superficial.

It is not only that nice things and bad things will happen to nice and bad people, it is *how* they will happen. Also, the "feeling of a controlling higher power" is a way of describing how these things happen. It is not a feeling like pain but a feeling like distrust that is assertive of the world and can be wise or foolish. The trouble with the objection is that it takes the analogies with dead unimaginative seriousness. The situation is reminiscent of that opposition to Freudian concepts of the unconscious which also took analogies too seriously. By demanding to know just where the analogies are to hold, the objectors to the Freudian concept of the unconscious and to the Christian concept of God try to impose what could only be an oversimplification. Also, they force the analogies to the point of ridicule—the giant figure behind the clouds, the little man within. Freudians and theologians not only make analogies in striking statements but say a great deal and give a great many examples that are relevant to the analogies. Looking at the analogies and not the examples can blind one to the real light they shed. Connections are made between occurrences we might mark by saying, "My baser self showed itself" and occurrences on the face of which there is no evidence of a baser self. This is done with the help of the unconscious self. Connections are made between the wisest and most foolish, poorest and richest, most civilized and most savage. This is done with the help of the Fatherhood of God.

It is true that we "can be no better off and *could* be no better off than we are for *really* finding God" if by this we mean finding or locating a something or somebody that can be called God. The difficulties of this have been found to be logically insuperable even in the case of Christ. But this does not mean that the analogy is useless or that there is no sense in being "better off" for "finding God" in the next life. There are marks that we all know for determining the presence of God and the work of the Devil in ourselves and in the world. These marks will be stronger. Occasionally, we feel that God takes a hand in human affairs. Sometimes we talk of a miracle. Sometimes justice is done unexpectedly and not decided upon or directed by any human agent.

# Religious Belief

Justice will be done in the next life and not decided upon or directed by human agents, and it will seem as if a judge had directed our reward and punishment on the basis of all that we had done and thought—an all-seeing, all-knowing, unprejudiced judge. The usefulness of speaking of God and employing the analogy of a Being operating behind the scene is here most pronounced. This may be compared with situations in which we feel inclined to speak of an unconscious wish, love, or hate, and then the situations may become exaggerated, as in automatic writing, when the usefulness of speaking of the unconscious and employing the analogy of a little man within is most pronounced. In neither of the extreme situations do we locate God or the unconscious self, but this does not denigrate the usefulness of these concepts in helping us to explain and to live in this world and the next. The pattern of the next life may "prove" the "existence" of God in the same way as automatic writing "proves" the "existence" of the unconscious self. The point is that life after death may better establish the "existence" of God than does this life, but it cannot establish it differently, and this is what the analogy sometimes suggests.

But now in all honesty I must warn the believer that this account affords him no sustenance. It is in essence an elaboration of the pseudopantheistic reduction discussed in the second chapter. It amounts to a reference to an organization and pattern of emphasis of facts about the world. The believer must now face the responsibility of answering the question "What more?" by more than a mere form of words.

# Seven

# Faith and Ritual

SOMETIMES religious people speak as if a man might have faith as a substitute for his statements having meaning. It is thought that the act of faith is a source and even a definitive source of knowledge. This claim must now be examined.

It is sometimes objected that religious faith is irrational because it goes against empirical evidence. Thus, faith in a good and powerful God is irrational because there is so much evil and suffering and waste in the world. The empirical evidence is against the assertion made by the faithful, and so the faithful are unreasonable in their faith. This objection is superficial and misguided.

It is superficial because it does violence to the notion of faith itself. This can be seen by considering cases of nonreligious faith. A coach may tell his team, "I have faith in you." He does not mean, "I think that you will win." In the case of the one statement the team's losing falsifies a prediction that proves false; with the other it does not. (Yet, as we shall see, there is a predictive element even here.) If the team makes a gallant effort and loses, and the coach discounts their courage, is willing to make no excuse or allowances for their defeat, then the team would be justified in feeling that he did not really have faith in them. Also, when X says of Y, "I have faith in him," and then proceeds to make no excuses or allowances for the misdeeds of Y, we are right in thinking that this is no instance of faith. Faith *must* display a resistance to contrary evidence. If one is to display faith, then one must not merely let the facts speak for themselves; one must commit oneself to interpreting the facts in a favorable light. "I have faith in his honesty" implies that the speaker should be more hesitant than the objective judge to place blame, believe stories of the man's dishonesty, find evidence of dishonesty, disclaim the man's plea of innocence. Faith may be irrational, but it need not be. A mother's faith in a wayward son, or a lover's faith in a faithless and worthless lover may show such resistance to counterevidence as to betray blindness and irrationality. But faith can be profoundly justified as well as blind. The commitment of trust and faith cannot be identical with inductive reasoning or prediction on the basis of the past and present. When a person has no faith in anyone else, we do not suspect him of unreasonableness but of moral callousness. Further, to have faith in oneself is to refuse to be discouraged by failure and to resist the conclusion that failure is the result of one's incapacity. This too can be stretched beyond the bounds of reason, but it need not be. After a lifetime of cowardice one can justify one's faith by a supreme act of moral courage. There is a fine sense of fulfillment when a hard-tested faith is finally justified. There is a terrible sense of loss when a hard-tested faith is finally proved to be without foundation.

A second and more profound objection to the notion of religious faith begins with an account of the misleadingness of the first objection. It is misleading to speak of religious faith running counter to empirical evidence, because this makes the statements of faith appear to be straightforwardly false. Nonreligious faith can be justified by certain events or shown to be unjustified by other events. There is a predictive or expectancy element that may or may not be clear-cut and explicit. Even in "Despite everything, I still have faith in his real goodness of heart," where the person has done nothing to justify the faith, it can be defended by "If only he had the right environment he would, etc." Also, if he is successful in the future or it is conceived how he *could* have been successful, this would be or would have been the justification. This is not and cannot be paralleled in religious faith. What would the justification of religious faith be like? We have images of the skies opening to us, of a celestial home-coming. None of this will do. An unredeemable promissory note concerning the future life is given us. This will not do. Whatever human conception produces is insufficient, and no directions are given for proceeding further than we have in fact proceeded. The answer "Wait and see" is not helpful if we have *no* idea of what this "seeing" might be like. To live on after death is one thing (and this idea is of overpowering difficulty), but to live on after death in such a way as would be a justification of one's faith in the existence of the perfectly good, omnipotent, omniscient Creator is still another sort of thing. It is this kind of justification that is unspecified and unspecifiable. Religious faith employs the model of a faith whose justification is conceivable, yet the model cannot apply in this most vital aspect. The model gives it meaning, and yet on the vital points it is withdrawn. Nothing is put in its place except "Wait and see," "One must not expect to apprehend the Infinite by finite means," and "Have faith." But, again we ask, "See what?" "Apprehend what?" "What would it be for this faith to be justified?" We cannot say that we fail in something if we cannot say and also rule out anyone else's saying what it would be like to succeed.

## Religious Belief

This critique can be strengthened by making a distinction between two kinds of faith which come together in religion. They are faith *in* someone and faith *that* something is the case. The religious person professes faith *that* God exists, *that* he has the infinite attributes of perfect goodness, wisdom, and power, and *that* he is the Creator of all things, and further *that* he was incarnate in Jesus Christ. The religious person also professes faith *in* God and his goodness and faith *in* Christ.

This distinction is *not* necessarily marked by any linguistic devices. "Faith in fairies" is a "faith *that*" in terms of the distinction made. "Faith that" refers to a story of some sort. In this sense then, when a person has faith in, or believes in, fairies, he believes that the stories told about fairies are true. When a child has faith that fairies exist and do the sorts of things described in the stories, he may derive this faith from his faith in, or belief in, or trust in, the person who tells him the stories. This "faith in" is a confidence in the goodness and trustworthiness of the person, which is not based purely on the record of past performance. To have faith in someone is not merely to believe that certain stories about him are true. This faith is of a personal nature and must arise out of one's acquaintance with the person.

The peculiarity of religious faith takes three forms. There is the peculiarity of the stories believed in "faith that," the peculiarity of the Storyteller *in* whom we have faith, and the peculiarity of our "acquaintance" with Him in whom we have faith. These three cannot be kept separate. Some of the stories are of overwhelming obscurity, such as that of the incarnation. These are totally beyond our conception. Other stories are not obscure, such as stories of the parting of the seas, the Voice in the burning bush, the child born of a virgin. These are within our conception. Or *are* they? Remember, the seas parted at the command of God, the Voice was God's, the child was the Son of God. Now, we look for the One who ordered, spoke, and fathered. Of course, we see nothing. Of course.

The religious person may now complain, "You look too much at the stories themselves. Of course, we do not know precisely in what way they refer to God, but you must remember that for the Christian the stories have weight only because of the storyteller. The stories are told by God through the media of his prophets and saints. It is our faith in him who tells the stories that convinces us of their truth and leaves us unshaken by our failure to make clear that truth."

If someone that I know well tells an incredible tale about something that happened of which he was the only witness, I may say, "If anyone else told me that, I should not believe it, but of course I take your word for it." I believe that the story is true because of my faith in my friend. But suppose that my friend tells an incredible tale about something that happened of which he was the only witness and then adds that the cause of the unlikely events was some indescribable agent. I may believe that something incredible but conceivable happened and also that my friend experienced something peculiar and difficult to express which drove him to speak of some sort of indescribable causal agent. My difficulty then is not in believing him but in understanding him, that is, in knowing just *what* to believe.

Sometimes this sort of difficulty does not concern us. Our belief often transcends our understanding, and we manage this by appeal to authority.[1] I may come to believe that my radio's queer behavior is caused by something with a technical-sounding name and have a very poor understanding of just what it is. I believe this because I think that the repairman is honest and knows about such things. The distance between belief and understanding becomes wider in the domains of higher mathematics and

---

[1] The notion of assertions exceeding understanding will be examined in detail in the next chapter.

science. My appeal to and trust in authority becomes quite desperate. I have little means of my own for deciding as to the truth or falsity of what is said, because I have such faltering understanding of what is said. However, the matter is not beyond the human court of appeal, and it is conceivable to me that I should come to lose faith in the authority upon whom I now depend. If my radio goes on behaving queerly despite the tinkering and technical analyses of the repairman, I shall give up believing what he says and shall not continue to repeat his fine-sounding diagnoses to my wife. If a mathematician or scientist loses the confidence of his colleagues and is branded as incompetent, I shall not continue to take his statements on trust. In these cases where faith in a person is so vital to belief in a statement it is fairly clear what sorts of things would disturb that faith. It is also fairly clear in the case of faith in my friend. Belief in his story would be destroyed if he were found out to be deceitful and untrustworthy.

All of this is true, but it does not help in the theological case. The implied and unexpressed analogies do not hold. The Authority is too different. God as the Storyteller is different in two vital and irreducible ways. The stories he tells are past the understanding of all creatures, for they involve him and his action. Also our faith in him is of a sort which implies no criteria for what would be or would not be its justification. Our faith in him and our belief in his stories are bound up together and are equally difficult.

Again, the religious person may complain, "You leave out something of great importance, namely, the personal relationship we have with God. Our acquaintance with God ultimately determines the nature of our faith in him." So the lover says, "If only you knew her as I do, you would have faith in her as I have." He reminds us of how love can be profound and perceptive as well as blind. It can be creative too. The love and faith of a child can make us more worthy of that love and faith. But that is another matter. We know about the personal relationship between lovers, friends, parents, and children. The procedures for getting acquainted with, and having a truly personal relationship with, people are known to us. We see people in many situations, when they are on their guard and when they are off their guard, at their best and at their worst, in all their moods, and we learn, by long watching and listening, to tell what they are thinking and feeling.

But what of God? There are procedures, of course. We read the Bible, worship, pray. But we do not learn by watching and listening. And it is not clear what it is we learn. The anger of God is the Divine Wrath; we are warned that it is only by analogy like the anger of men, and we are never told where the analogy holds. The love of God is the Divine Love; we are warned that it is only by analogy like the love of men, and we are never told where the analogy holds. Or perhaps we are told that it is a love that works for our welfare. Then something terrible happens to us, and we are told that God's love "passeth all understanding."

But was there not once a more direct procedure for a personal relationship with God? Christ walked and talked with men. He had his moods, and the disciples came to know when he was tired and discouraged, and they often felt the sting of his disapproval and impatience. All this is told so graphically in the Gospels that we must feel that we too know Christ. Their personal relationship with him as man, worker of miracles, the crucified and raised from the dead, presents no conceptual difficulty. But the real difficulty rests in how the disciples' personal relationship with Christ was with him as *God*. We have discussed the difficulties of this conception in Chapter Four.

This brings us to the end of the second objection. I believe that it is not wrong and is an excellent corrective, but it is unsympathetic. What has been done must not be forgotten, but we must start again in a new direction.

A distinction must be made between two kinds of statements employed in religious language. I shall call these two types of statements statements *in the faith* and statements *outside the faith*.

When a man speaks in the faith, he speaks ritualistically. The matter, form, and tone of his answers to questions posed are set, and to depart from these in any substantial way is for him to speak not only falsely or inappropriately but also blasphemously. Further, the matter, form, and tone of what he says is not of his own choosing: he takes them to be ordained by God. More will be said about this later. Take the following dialogue as an example of a man speaking in the faith.

A: "Is there a God?"

B: "Certainly."

A: "But what do you mean by God?"

B: "The perfectly good, wise, powerful, eternal Creator of all things."

A: "What do you mean by all of that?"

B: "Just what I said—the perfectly good, wise . . ."

A: "Yes, yes. But these words mean very little to me."

B: "Then read the Bible, worship, pray, and learn of Christ."

This is not a debate. "Him that is weak in the faith receive ye, but not to doubtful disputations" (Rom. 14:1).

I am not in the least interested in whether or not anyone ever does speak only in the faith and never outside the faith. The point I want to stress is that there are two different ways of speaking in religious language. When a man speaks outside the faith, he does not speak ritualistically. One can debate with him and call what he says in question, and he cannot employ the authority of God for what he says. He enters the lists when he accepts our challenge to explain what he means, to give arguments for what he says in the faith. He may be unclear, unreasonable, and confused—he is vulnerable, or his statements are vulnerable, to the test of reason. When a man speaks in the faith and will not step outside, we feel that we are battling with air.

I spoke of the ritualism of statements made in the faith in order to liken them to the actual rites of religious ceremony. The time has come to speak of the nature of ritual behavior, linguistic and nonlinguistic.

The utterance of certain statements is doing what the statements claim to do. "I promise," "With this ring I thee wed," "With all my worldly goods I thee endow" are examples. The rites in religious ceremony have this character. An example would be "We bless Thee, we praise Thee, we magnify Thee, we give thanks unto Thee." Saying these things is taking action. When such utterances are religious, the action is prescribed by Divine Authority.

Related to this type of statement is another. A child says of a table, "This is my wigwam." He does not mean by this simply, "Since I haven't a wigwam, this will have to serve instead." And certainly the child is not speaking falsely when he makes the statement. He is defining the nature of the thing for the purpose of what he is to do with it in this particular context of his game. For him now it *is* a wigwam, and it is *not* an article of furniture. The mother who says, "Get up off the floor this minute and sit up at the table!" spoils the game not only by her temper but also by her insistence upon the nature of the table as a prosaic article of furniture serving certain restrictive purposes. The table cannot be at one and the same time for one and the same person wigwam and furniture. Christ said of the bread as he broke it, "This is my body, broken for you." I do not mean to be sacrilegious when I liken this to the game of the child. People have confused themselves when they have thought that this must be taken literally or metaphorically or symbolically. Literally, it is false, metaphorically, it is ridiculous. Symbolically, it loses force. When the child said, "This is my wigwam," he did not speak falsely, and he did not mean that the table was *like* a wigwam, and he did not mean to use it in place of one. He meant that for him now and in the context of his game this was a wigwam. Saying so makes it so. It is an act of creation. If one now says that it is all a matter of the imagination, this degrades the reality the situation has for the child and dismisses the character of what is actually done with the table. His behavior has a certain form and seriousness. He plays the game seriously (and this does not mean lack of gaiety) and wholeheartedly in a way which an adult finds difficult. (To substitute a real wigwam for the table is not to improve but to change the nature of the game.)

A father who pretends he doesn't know what is in the parcel his child has given him feels as if he doesn't know, feels as if he is guessing, feels as if he thought it might be alive and bite him. But he doesn't really think it might be alive, he really knows that it's chocolate, he's only pretending to wonder what it is. But since he *pretends to himself* that he doesn't know *is* he only pretending? Shall we say that for the moment he forgets he knows, that for the moment he wonders? When he turns quickly to fire on the wolves who are gaining in spite of the efforts of two exhausted rocking chairs, he is really excited. He is pretending that wolves are behind but he isn't pretending he thinks that wolves are behind. He feels that they are, he sort of believes they are, he half believes it. No, it isn't that he half believes it, he doesn't. It is more that just for the moment he believes it. The illusion is fragile. It breaks if you touch it. At least it does if you touch it with an unsympathetic hand.[2]

---

[2] John Wisdom, *Other Minds* (Oxford: Basil Blackwell, 1952), pp. 22–23.

## Faith and Ritual

The religious person who hears the words repeated, "This is my body," and takes the bread does all of this in a way not possible for the nonreligious person. (To substitute somehow the actual flesh and blood body of Christ would not improve but utterly change the nature of the ritual.) He is acting in the faith. More must be said about acting, verbally and not verbally, in the faith.

It is helpful to compare the ritual of religious behavior with that of certain kinds of nonreligious behavior. The set form of a dance of victory may have arisen from what was once spontaneous capering and is now considered fitting to the occasion. This form distinguishes this dance from others and ties it to occasions of victory in the past and present. Of course, this is a primitive ritual and a far cry from the Mass. What is to be said and done, left unsaid and not done, has been developed over a long period, and those most capable of judging determine what is fitting. Sometimes directly and sometimes indirectly the ordination of religious ceremony comes from God. Christ said, "This do in remembrance of me."

As the form of a ceremony crystallizes, it achieves a kind of universality. Having the sanction of tradition, it is felt at each particular performance of the standard ritual that, being the same in form as all other past performances, the present instance is not just another occasion on which a well-tried formula best expresses the present mood of a community. Rather it is through the retention of one traditional form that all various occasions, differing widely in place and date and performers, become a unity within which each occasion is a part of the whole pattern. In this way, a nation uses its traditional ceremonies (coronation service) not merely as a well-tried formula for the expression of that which is felt by all or most members of the nation on such an occasion but also to give a sense of national

131

unity with the past and future. It is in this way too that religious people are able to regard the occasions of their ceremonies as one and the same whenever and wherever they are carried out. Catholics do not merely say that each day's Mass is a new instance of an old form, though of course temporally it is, but also affirm that each celebration of Mass not merely commemorates but is identical with the historical self-sacrifice of the Cross. Such an identification with that which in place and time is distinct is possible only through the form.

The type of performance we are considering may be called "the celebration." The word here does not necessarily carry any felicitous significance. Deaths are celebrated as well as births, marriages, victories. There is a universal form involving a hearse, feast, or whatever. There may be celebrations once and for all, as one specific event—the single occasion of celebrating this death, marriage, or the like. There is another kind of celebration which is intended from the first not to be a solitary occasion but to be repeated perhaps in perpetuity at stated intervals. When a ceremony is ordained to be repeated in this way without any period or term fixed for its cessation, it has already taken on a new significance. If it is not purely personal to specific individuals and therefore not to stop at their death, if it expresses something of significance to a whole community, if it is ordained that it be done daily, monthly, yearly, forever, then it thereby symbolizes in some sense the aspiration of that community to live, somehow, forever.

Ceremonial behavior is not random, and it is not purposeless. There is an answer to the questions "Why is this done?" and "What is being celebrated?" In religion the account of that which is celebrated is a story, in some cases a myth, which the faithful have been taught before they actually perform the acts of celebration.

What is the difference between a mythological story and a

fairy story? The two are utterly distinct in their nature and purpose, and those who have dismissed mythology and, indeed, Christian revelation as if they had the same type of function as a child's story have seriously misunderstood the nature of the former. The world of fairy tale is a world of make-believe. It is a free creation of the imagination. It is a world in which a man may turn from the frustration and pain and harsh realities of the real world, and, so long as the illusion is maintained, he can find compensation in the dream world in which wishes are fulfilled and all is governed by his own desires. The myth is not a free imaginative creation without any firm connection with reality. On the contrary, it sets out to represent in symbolic form the nature of the world and the place of man within it. Tragic themes recur, and victory comes at high cost. Danger, pain, suffering, and death are often pictured as adversaries of man or the hero representing man. Battle with the powers of darkness, determination to win life by the conquest of suffering and death, and final victory are often represented by the hero's winning for himself and his people the gift of immortality, and this at terrible cost. The myth sets out to present a picture of the world and to symbolize the realities of human life. It does not, like the fairy tale, aim at entertainment or at evoking the comforts of wishful thinking. On the contrary, it succeeds or fails in representing the world. Further, it is profound or superficial in its representation. The richness and profundity of the Christian story is limitless. It is this that the man who acts and speaks in the faith is aware of and in which he is secure. What he has seems inexhaustible and all-sufficient. His ceremonial behavior keeps this continually alive for him. Our academic questionings may move him little.

A further point of contrast between myth and fairy tale is that fairy tales are not inconsistent with one another, whereas myths may be. For the Christian there is only one story of

God's action that is true, and stories that do not agree with this are false.

The problem of how the Christian story can be said to be true or false may engage us though not the man in the faith. This does not mean that the same man cannot make statements both inside and outside the faith. It means that statements made in the faith have a certain security. So long as a man remains in the faith, he has sanctuary from the probings of philosophical debate. This security may be called by some "false" and "irrational." This likens it to the dogmatism of political and moral opinion in which the dogmatist asserts his position but will not consider rationally arguments brought against it. The security may be called by others "religious" and "faithful." This contrasts it with all forms of dogmatism in which the assertions are not claimed to have divine ordination and suggests a world of spiritual wealth and fullness of life denied to the outsider. The answer to the question "How shall a man live?" is given "He shall live in the faith." The ritual of Christian behavior should extend into every part of one's life. It is to play the life-and-death game of acting as if by the will of another. In the words of the apostle, "I live, yet no longer I, but Christ in me."

The theologian is something of a figure of fun as he steps outside the faith to explain and defend the faith against argument and, speaking of "analogies" or "the limitation of human reason," jumps back inside. The greater his nimbleness at leaping the boundary of faith, the more comic he is, and the more force have the words of St. Paul, "Him that is weak in the faith receive ye, but not to doubtful disputations." Yet the security of being in the faith is gained at a very high cost. This chapter has been critical of statements in the faith. It is a challenge. If the challenge is ignored, then honesty demands that these statements be intellectually suspect. The answer to the question "How shall a man live?" can still be given "He shall live in the faith," but then perhaps we would feel that this would be to live a lie.

# Eight

# "Beyond All Human Understanding"

ONE of the most important ideas underlying theological language is that assertion can exceed understanding. It is thought that by means of faith and revelation one can and must make assertions about the Divine Mysteries (the ultimate nature of God's being, the Trinity, and so on) that exceed one's finite understanding. Can one delegate (to God or someone else) the responsibility for the meaning of one's own statements?

Sometimes the theologian claims that theological assertions may exceed human understanding and contradict the logic of finite reason.

Hence God can never be found along any way of thought; for indeed this idea of God bursts through and destroys all the fundamental categories of thought: the absolutely antithetical character of the basic logical principles of contradiction and identity. To want to *think* this God for oneself would mean insanity.[1]

This somewhat casual attitude toward "the basic logical principles of contradiction and identity" allows the same author in the same book to make the contradictory claim that theological assertions may exceed human understanding but must *not* contradict the logic of finite reason.

Within the truth of revelation all that reason knows and recognizes falls into place. The truth of revelation is not in opposition to any truth of reason, nor to any fact that has been discovered by the use of reason. Genuine truths of faith are never in conflict with logic or with the sciences; they conflict only with the rationalistic or positivistic metaphysics, that is with a reason that arrogates to itself the right to derive the whole range of truth from the standpoint of *man.*[2]

There is no argument against the first position stated by Brunner. It is its own *reductio ad absurdum.*

The second position stated by Brunner is the one with which we shall be concerned in what follows. Its exponents have been various and number Luther, Calvin, St. Thomas, Augustine, and most other Christian theologians of the first rank. Newman says, "Unless Thou wert incomprehensible Thou wouldst not be God." Augustine writes, "What, then are we to say of God? If you have understood what you are trying to say, it is not God. If you have been able to understand it, it is something other than God that you have understood." St. Thomas writes, "Having arrived at the term of our knowledge we know God as unknown: and our mind penetrates in a perfect way into the knowledge of God *precisely when* it knows that the divine essence is above all that our mind can grasp in this life."

---

[1] Emil Brunner, *Revelation and Reason* (London: S. C. M. Press, 1947), p. 47.
[2] *Ibid.,* p. 213.

## Religious Belief

Let us first consider this matter outside the theological context. (The argument of this chapter, so far as any argument is relevant, is an answer to those who will try to discredit all that I have said by insisting that my criteria for determining what is meaningful are "narrow and positivistic.")

Suppose that a group of people live their entire lives in a cave and limited by their chains never have a glimpse of the outside world. Shadows of passing things are projected upon the wall of the cave. Because of the peculiarity of the light nothing within the cave casts a shadow; otherwise there would be an available analogy that would spoil the point of this case. One of the group remarks, "I think our apprehension of reality is limited and we do not know things as they really are." When his companions question him as to what it would be like to apprehend reality, he is unable to answer. They complain that he has given no meaning to this "lack" which he asserts, because he can establish no contrast between lack and fulfillment. To assert a deficiency meaningfully one must be able to say something about a possible state of affairs that would remove this deficiency. When this is not done, the man who claims deficiency merely employs a form of words but by his assertion does not make any difference for us between deficiency and fulfillment. His utterance does not have the meaning the form of words suggests until he can make that difference.[3]

A passer-by may overhear the cave dweller and think, "He's quite right. They mistake shadow for reality." This man, by making the needful contrast, gives meaning to the cave dweller's utterance. Notice this. The utterance as made did not *have* meaning but was *given* meaning. In the same way, I may say, "Ips comsupst mebow," and, though as used by me the words have no meaning, someone on another planet may note my

---

[3] It will become clear later how this is too harsh and stringent a demand.

138

words and say, "He's quite right. It is raining." What does what another can do with my words have to do with that which I wish to assert or not to assert by means of them?

This passer-by may return to his community and tell what happened, saying, "Might not we be somehow in a similar position and in some way continually mistaking appearance for reality?" His form of words suggests that he has made an analogy and thereby has made a reference to a possible state of affairs. When he is questioned just *how* he and his fellows might be in a similar position to the cave dwellers, he is as unable to say as were the cave dwellers he overheard. He too has given no meaning to his statement, because he has made no contrast between "appearance" and "reality." However, he may have good or bad answers to this objection, and, until these answers are seen and considered, the point of the metaphysical theological doctrine of assertion exceeding understanding and meaning will remain hidden. He may answer, "I cannot say what apprehending reality would be like, but just as I could speak where the cave dwellers couldn't, so someone who has resources I do not have (God perhaps) may be able to say and explain what I, limited as I am, cannot. Thus that person could see how my statement (which I cannot explain) is in fact true."

But has a statement, true or false, been made? If we allow a statement or assertion to be a form of words that can be *given* sense, then any collection of words is a statement or assertion. For even if they are not used in such a way that they have sense, they *could* be so used. The point is, has the person so used them that they have the required sense? That is, is he able in his use to make the sort of contrast between "appearance" and "reality" that is needed for his assertion to be true or false? It is *his* assertion that we are considering and not the possible assertions of others employing his form of words.

He may answer again, "Your stricture 'no contrast, no meaning' is too severe. After all, if the cave dweller had known what I knew (had been able to see outside the cave), he would have said 'That is what I meant.' You speak as if his words were totally arbitrary and empty. I am suggesting that someone might know something or that there should be a state of affairs such that if I learned it I should say, 'That is what I meant.' " In the religious context it is as if the religious believer is suggesting that such a state of affairs (confronting the Infinite Omnipotent God) in some afterlife might obtain that he could turn to me in triumph and say, "That is what I meant!"

This complaint should force us to a more careful and sympathetic approach than has so far been given. We must come to an understanding of just how one can mean more than one can say.

Let us return to the man who overheard the cave dwellers and who sought in his own situation and society to make an analogy that he could not explain between his society and that of the cave dwellers. Can we dismiss his words as totally arbitrary and empty, wholly without function?

We have demanded a contrast (between appearance and reality) that he cannot give. This is a serious weakness. Yet making a meaningful assertion is a complicated kind of behavior, and our criterion in this case, "No contrast, no meaning," is oversimplified. He is doing something with these words, for, at the least, his words give expression to a feeling of uncertainty and uneasiness about the world. (So too does the religious man give expression to a whole complex of feelings and ways of looking at the world, some of them common to most of us some of the time. How much more he accomplishes with his statements and religious form of behavior is the problem of this book.) The cave dweller gives voice to the warning, "Don't be surprised if the world plays you false in ways you don't expect." So, now our claim is that his statement has no *further* meaning. Or, of course, he might mean that not any of us knows everything. This is a rather cheap way of laying claim to newly discovered truths.

It is tempting to think that if anything is meant in such a case there must be some implicit reference to one particular state of affairs (in the cave case, seeing how shadows are not things, but are shadows of things) for the description of which our language and experience is unfortunately unprepared. This reference seems both essential and miraculous.

We get a kind of smoke screen which blurs the edges of this dilemma when religious thinkers suggest that in this matter we are rather like children. The finite mind (like that of a child) can only make inadequate reference, but reference still, to things infinite (adult affairs). The strength of this persistent analogy is that it is hard even for a child to mean nothing by what he says. But we are concerned with how far the child employs his words to mean what the adult means. For just so far does he share the adult's assertion. Of course, it is easy for the child to share a form of words long before he is in a position to employ them to make anything like the adult's assertion. Crude instruments of meaning detection such as the positivist's verification principle fail to register the delicacies, because they have no means of registering how coming to make a given assertion or learning the meaning of a word are matters of degree. As children and as adults we are often on the way long before we arrive. However, the fault of this analogy is irremediable. The fact that the adult makes an assertion by means of certain words is of no concern to us when we examine what the child is doing with those same words. The adult cannot by the exercise of parental authority guarantee that the child's uttering the words is not merely obedient mouthing but making an assertion. Whether or not the child makes or comes close to making an assertion depends upon what *he,* and not the parent, can do with the words. It is for this reason that *when the meaning of religious utterances is in question, no appeal can be made to revelation or external authority. These become relevant only when the question of meaning is settled and the question of belief arises.*

A way out of the dilemma of a miraculous yet seemingly essential reference may be found by considering a quite different range of examples. Sometimes we are searching for a word to describe some happening, and someone says something and we exclaim, "Yes, that is what I meant." Here is a clear case of meaning more than one can (at the moment) say. The only trouble with it is that it is too clear to help with our present problem. For it is only a trick of memory that kept one from saying what one meant to say. There is more to it than that in the cases we are considering. For we want to say two things: firstly, that it is a failure of understanding and not of memory; secondly, that this failure of understanding does not keep us from saying something about how we may be deceived in ways we do not understand concerning the world (compare the cave dweller), or prevent us from asserting something about the incomprehensibly good, powerful, all-creating, all-sustaining God.

The kind of example that comes nearest to what we want is that of a "hunch." A young and largely untrained scientist may get a hunch that some sort of theory could explain and relate a host of hitherto unrelated facts. He certainly cannot say what such a theory would be, though he confidently asserts that there is one and that his problem is to find it. His present technical competence is so inadequate that if someone were to present him with the theory he would be incapable of understanding it. But from the beginning his inquiry has a direction and

### "Beyond All Understanding"

point.[4] After years of training and much thought the theory suddenly comes to him. He could say, "That is what I meant all along." There is a sense in which he could not have meant this all along. That is, at the time of his hunch his understanding was inadequate to the task of asserting or making sense of the theory he later produced. Yet there is also a sense in which he did mean it all along and would have meant it even if he never became capable of understanding it. That sense is that his thought and investigations have a certain direction. *This direction of thought and inquiry remains even if his hope of finding the theory is based upon confusion and muddle.*

The religious believer may feel impatient here. He not only wants more than this but he very likely will claim that he has more. For he will claim to understand in part though not in full his religious utterances. One should be grateful for all the meaning one can get in this context, and I wish to reject none. We are supposed to be really informed concerning God's attributes by the example of Christ's life. If that is so, then we have the notion of God as of very considerable moral stature, far greater in degree than that of any man. We feel that God, being good, would never cause injury to anyone *just* because he wanted to (though sometimes people speak as if his goodness were compatible with doing such a vicious thing—see the discussion on pages 30–31 above). Anything that is within human understanding is to be included in the concept of God, and anything that is beyond human understanding plays no part in the assertions of human beings. In this book I have limited myself to the examination of human utterances.

There is one more sort of case relevant to the desire to speak

---

[4] Note that even should someone else's (a superscientist's perhaps) language and experience be prepared for the formulation of this theory, the young scientist's are not, and it is *his* assertion and situation we are considering just as it is the theologian's or religious believer's assertion and situation with which we are concerned.

as if assertion can exceed understanding. There are times when we very naturally feel that a set of words carries a meaning that we understand only in part. We may feel that their full significance eludes us. This feeling is encouraged if the person who speaks or writes these words is known to be of greater intelligence and insight than we are ourselves. Our task then would be to find the full meaning, and we may be inadequate to this task.

The significance and meaning of the very greatest works of literature often seem well nigh inexhaustible. These works have the power to evoke emotional responses of a complexity and subtlety that seems without limit. As we grow in sensitivity and emotional maturity, so our responses to them grow in depth and in ways that no other words can ever fully describe. Indeed, the original words do not describe these responses; instead they uniquely evoke them. Religious utterances in the Bible and the set forms of ritual have this power. But of course there is much more than this, and what should concern us is that which takes the form and to some degree the content of assertion.

Some of the dialogues of Plato and some of the plays of Shakespeare contain more significance than we have yet fathomed. The meaning lies somehow in the words, partly exposed and partly buried. And it is not necessarily the case that Plato and Shakespeare themselves could reveal or be aware of all that lies beneath the surface. For great writers often by their words suggest to others more than they themselves fully understand, though I do not mean by this to claim that they write their works by chance. But their works are a public property, and if they are not to die their significance depends upon what their words suggest to succeeding ages. There is much that can be understood at a glance. The plot and character situation in a Shakespearian play are easily understood at an elementary level.

## *"Beyond All Understanding"*

What is suggested by their means is limitless. Plato's myth of the cave is easily understood at an elementary level. What it suggests is perhaps inexhaustible. The facts of Christ's simple stories as found in the Bible can be understood by a child. What they suggest is without limit. It is such cases as these that give point to thinking of the meaning and significance as somehow being in the words and awaiting revelation. Yet this point is of no help to him who thinks he can make assertions in excess of his understanding.

What I mean and what assertion I make by means of a form of words is what they suggest to me and what I can do with them. What they suggest to others has to do with their assertions and not mine. The religious believer wants by some form of words (for example, "God is love") to make *his* assertion such that it exceeds *his* understanding. I have tried to show how this is a mistake, and I have tried to reveal some of its sources.

There is much that we do not know, and there is much that we do not understand. There are mysteries beyond number that the limits of our understanding will not allow us to fathom. But this surely is no place for disagreement between the theist and the atheist.

# Nine

# "Why is there anything at all?"

A consideration of the nature of religious belief forces us to the limits of our understanding. The theistic hypothesis is an answer to the question "What are our most ultimate explanations of how the world is as it is?" If this is not in all ways a bogus question, we must compare the religious hypothesis with other possible hypotheses. The conceptual difficulties in our way are legion. Part of the strength of the theistic hypothesis is the difficulty of thinking clearly concerning any alternative cosmological theory.

## I

If we are forced to consider the character of cosmological forms of explanation, it is essential that we should come to grips with some aspects of the notion of time. Is time infinite or finite? A child can feel puzzlement here. It seems both that there must and must not be limits.

We may be inclined to think that if there were no events and no things "time" would have no use, indeed, no meaning. We decide intervals of time by the dating of certain events. There is no other way. Suppose we trace past intervals by referring to past events until we come to a time in which there is an event before which there are no things and no happenings. We can say that this is the beginning of things and the beginning of time. This can be said only because there is a sense of "time" in which it would be impossible to say that time had a beginning. For consistent with this case is the *possibility* that there should have been further happenings (after the last in our series) without limit. This possibility is the sense of infinite time. We do seem to be compelled to think of a time before the first happening, whereas we do not need to think of a happening preceding the first. If asked to talk about that time in which there was nothing, we can do so only in terms of possible events, but then we may feel that it is not something to talk about or describe. Time is neither a thing nor an event: it is not even a number of these.

Whatever may be truly said in cosmology will be wonderful. Whether the world has a beginning, by some external agency [1] or none, or whether the world has no beginning, it is a place for wonder.

If we date backwards in terms of actual events or duration of things, either (a) there comes a time before which there was nothing or (b) there is no time before which there was nothing. If someone were to claim that he did not understand what I meant by (a), I should find it hard to believe him, and I would suspect him of trying to picture this state of affairs—would the emptiness be white or grey or black? It seems meaningful to say that the world consists of just five stars and nothing else, or if you like, nothing but space and time. It seems meaningful to say that these stars pass out of existence one at a time. When the last

---

[1] There is a sense in which such an agency cannot be external to the world. This will be discussed later.

star passes out of existence, there is nothing at all or, if you like, nothing but space and time. If there was a time before which there was nothing, it would be wonderful that things should come to be at all. This would be a state of affairs that cried out for and yet defied explanation. I think, however, that it is not a logical impossibility or a meaningless supposition.

If (b) is true, this is wonderful also. For if there is no time before which there was nothing, then either some one thing or being (God perhaps) or some one "happening" (God's love of himself perhaps) or set of things or happenings, has infinite past duration. Or at any time in the past there has been an infinite number of things and happenings. The notion of an infinite number of things or happenings in the past may give us a twinge of uneasiness that we would not have concerning the notion of an infinite number of things or happenings in the future. This uneasiness may be caused by our feeling that the past is a completed series and the future is not. This is a mistake. The past is no more begun than the future is ended. The place to begin an infinite series in the future is any moment you choose after the present. The place to begin an infinite series in the past is any moment you choose before the present. In neither case would the series be concluded. There is no more difficulty in the idea of an infinite number of past things or happenings than in the idea of an infinite number of future things or happenings. The alternative is to say that at some time in the past things *must* start and at some time in the future things *must* stop.

The theistic hypothesis asserts (b). At no time was there nothing because there has always been God. According to St. Thomas, following Aristotle, it is possible that at any time there should have been something (finite in duration) other than God, and it is therefore possible that there should have been an infinite number of such things. St. Thomas asserts that it is only by revelation and not by reason that we know that this is not the case.

## "Why is there anything?"

What St. Thomas claims to prove by reason is that one and only one being could exist from the beginning of time and depend upon nothing else for its existence. He claims to prove more, but this is an important part of what he claims to prove. I shall discuss this in detail later.

St. Thomas' arguments for the existence of God provide us with the richest material for philosophical analysis. However, I shall not discuss these arguments in detail. Instead, I shall try to sort out two lines of thought that can be found in the arguments with special reference to the third argument. One line of thought is a muddle. The other is not, and though it is not established by the arguments it is of considerable interest. The critics of St. Thomas have called attention to the muddle only. I shall quote only the third argument.

The third way is taken from possibility and necessity, and runs thus. We find in nature things that are possible to be and not to be, since they are found to be generated, and to corrupt, and consequently, they are possible to be and not to be. But it is impossible for these always to exist, for that which is possible to be at some time is not. Therefore, if everything is possible not to be, then at one time there could have been nothing in existence. Now if this were true, even now there would be nothing in existence, because that which does not exist only begins to exist by something already existing. Therefore, if at one time nothing was in existence, it would have been impossible for anything to have begun to exist; and thus even now nothing would be in existence—which is absurd. Therefore, not all beings are merely possible, but there must exist something the existence of which is necessary. But every necessary thing either has its necessity caused by another, or not. Now it is impossible to go on to infinity in necessary things which have their necessity caused by another, as has been already proved in regard to efficient causes. Therefore we cannot but postulate the existence of some being having of itself its own necessity, and not receiving it from another, but rather causing in others their necessity. This all men speak of as God.[2]

Misinterpretation is so common that it is necessary to insist that St. Thomas nowhere rests his argument upon the impossibility of an infinite series of finite, contingent things. He does rest his argument on what he takes to be the impossibility of either a finite or infinite series of such things in the absence of an infinite, necessary being.

Just why we cannot proceed to infinity, is because there must be a sufficient reason, a cause. Even if we could go back to infinity in a series of past accidental causes, as, for instance, transformations of energy, or of generations of living beings, or of human beings: movement, life, the human soul would still have to be explained. These accidental causes are in themselves insufficient, and demand a further explanation. To carry the series to infinity would not change their nature. As Aristotle remarked: If the world is eternal, it is eternally insufficient and incomplete; it eternally demands a sufficient reason for its reality and intelligibility. (Met., I. XII, c. 6.) [3]

The Thomistic picture is not that of a finite or infinite number of billiard balls putting one another successively in motion. Rather is it of higher and higher levels of explanation.

If the proof by efficient cause rests, . . . on the impossibility of an infinite regression in the causal series, it is because, here again, some essentially ordered causes are hierarchically ordered causes. An infinite series of causes of the same degree is not only possible, but even, on the Aristotelian hypothesis of the eternity of the world, necessary. . . . The first term contains in its essence virtually the causality of the entire series and of each of the terms

---

[2] Aquinas, *Summa Theologica*, Part 1, Q2, Art. 3. Reprinted from the *Summa Theologica*, Benziger Brothers, Inc., publishers and copyright owners in the United States.

[3] Reginald Garrigou-Lagrange, *God: His Existence and His Nature* (St. Louis: Herder Book Co., 1955), I, 80–81.

that constitute it. . . . There is not only one efficiency, but there is only one single source of efficiency for the whole world.[4]

What I take to be a muddle in the Thomist arguments for the existence of God may best be brought out by considering the "third way" argument which I have already quoted. St. Thomas claims that:

1. If a thing is possible to be and not to be, then at some time that thing is not.

2. If everything is possible not to be, then at some time nothing was in existence.

3. If anything comes into existence, then something else brought it into existence.

4. If at some time nothing was in existence, then nothing would now exist.

5. Since something does now exist, there must exist a Being for whom it is not possible for it not to exist.

It is hard to see how St. Thomas came to assert (1). Surely not every possibility must be actualized. It is possible that at a particular time someone should stand and it is possible that he should remain seated. Both are possible, but only one can be actualized. What we assert to be possible is what we can *understand* as a possible happening whether it does or does not happen. Since (2) depends upon (1), it is equally questionable.

The only trouble with (3) is that it is not a demonstrable truth, and even if asserted it needs (1) and (2) to work as an argument for a necessary being. The difficulty with (5) is not only that it follows from untrue and muddled premises, but that it suggests that God's existence is logically necessary. That is, it suggests that it does not make sense to say that it is possible that God should not exist. But, surely, we can *understand* what it would be like for God not to exist. For we can conceive of what

---

[4] Translated by the author from Etienne Gilson, *Le Thomisme* (Paris: Libraire Philosophique J. Vrin, 1944), p. 101.

it would be like for nothing to exist. What we can understand is a possibility.

Does it follow from this that there is no kind of necessity that could be proper to God? I think not. But we must work to this concept of "necessity" by trying to see how explanations are ultimate. We may then find a sense for an "ultimate being."

## II

It will be of help to sort out three sorts of explanations.

1. Historical explanation.

By "historical explanation" I mean an explanation that involves a causal series which may or may not have a limit. A is the parent of B, and C is the parent of B, and D is the parent of C, etc., etc.

"Why did the glass fall?"

"Because the table moved."

"Why did the table move?"

"Because the house shook."

"Why . . . ?"

Such a series of answers can go on without limit or stop with the beginning of things.

2. Purposive explanation.

Explanation of a course of events in terms of someone's purpose, reason, or motive [5] can *not* go on and on without limit.

"Why did you smash the glass?"

"Because I wanted to."

"Why did you want to?"

"Because I wanted to attract the waiter's attention."

"Why?"

"Because I was hungry and wanted him to bring food."

Of course, there may be a further reason, motive or purpose

---

[5] I think there is no reason to go into the differences between these three concepts here.

underlying this, but there comes a point where there is none. This does not mean that after one stops one cannot go on with an historical-causal explanation.

The purposive kind of explanation does not explain (as it may seem to do) by relating the falling glass event to some sort of mental event of wanting or purposing. If it did, it would not be different from the causal kind of explanation. One would then have to show that when mental events of this kind are present glasses fall. But this is a ridiculous picture of the situation. It suggests an inner urge in oneself that sets the world in motion. We sit there vibrating inwardly, mentally, and as a result the glass falls to the ground. Mind over Matter! This is not what we mean when we explain why things happen in the world by reference to our wants and wishes and purposes. The picture is no better if we think of it as an inner urge (wanting, purposing) setting my arm in motion so as to strike the glass. For this too would be merely an implausible causal account.

Purposive or motive explanation is of its own kind and is not reducible to causal explanation. If an explanation of a course of events is given in terms of someone's purpose or motive and if it is not to be thought of as a purposive event setting other events in motion, what is it? It is an account in terms of the *character* of a person's thought and action, and this is to be found not only in his actual thought and action but also in how he is disposed to think and act.

"Why is the furniture smashed?"

"Because Mary turned him down."

Here there is a complicated but completely understandable reference to how the wishes, wants and purposes of someone can have a disastrous effect upon furniture. We can all fill in the story. If we could not then it would not be an explanation for us. The question to answer is, "How did his actions come to bear on the course of events we are trying to explain *in such a way* that we are justified in saying that these events occurred as a result of certain of his wants, desires, and purposes?" The answer to such a question cannot remain in total obscurity without the purposive explanation losing point. This may be put in a general form in the following way. Where we explain a course of events in terms of certain motives or purposes of an agent, we must be able to conceive of what it was about the action of the agent that warrants such explanation; otherwise there is no difference between asserting and denying the explanation, and so it is vacuous.

3. Theoretical explanation.

Theoretical explanation of a course of events may have higher and higher levels of generality and abstractness.

"Why did the glass break?"

"It is fragile." This explanation involves a generalization open to nontechnical observation.

"Why is it fragile?"

"The molecular structure is [physical or technical description]."

"Why is the molecular structure this way?"

"The atomic [subatomic, subsubatomic]. . . ."

I want very much to say that explanation of this sort must stop somewhere. And I want to say that the stopping is not merely a practical or arbitrary device. I do not know how to prove this. I shall have to content myself with trying to show the possibility of a nonarbitrary stopping place. The urge to say we *must* stop somewhere is what cosmological forms of argument for the existence of God feed upon. It is relevant then to ask what such a stopping place would be like.

An ultimate or basic law of nature would be one that would hold at all times and places and would not be deducible from any other law of nature of greater abstractness or generality. It is clear that we should never be in enough times and places to reach

## "Why is there anything?"

any final confirmation that we had successfully formulated such a basic law, though we could easily find something that would confute it. I see no reason to doubt that our assertions can extend beyond the possibility of final confirmation. I may assert, "He will *never* stop talking," and what I mean is something whose final confirmation is self-contradictory. There is as well the practical observation that physics is always changing, and it would be a dangerous conceit at any time to claim with assurance that we had come upon a set of basic laws or a single basic law. This does not militate against the possibility of such laws.

Yet even if such a law is possible it could not satisfy the theologian with whom we are dealing. "This law of the conservation of energy is not a necessary truth, a supreme law which nature is compelled to obey; itself contingent, it demands a cause." [6] Here, the sense of "contingent" seems clear. It seems to mean "true as a matter of fact and not true by logical necessity." What is contingently true we can conceive to have been otherwise. To ask of an account of how the world is as it is that it should be true by logical necessity is to ask the logically impossible. Yet the desire to ask this is to some degree understandable.

If a law is really a basic one, any request for an explanation of it is self-contradictory. To explain a law is to place it in a context or network of wider and more inclusive laws; a basic law is by definition one of which this cannot be done. . . . Like so many others, this point may seem logically compelling but psychologically unsatisfying. Having heard the above argument, one may still feel inclined to ask, "Why are the basic uniformities of the universe the way they are, and not some other way? Why should we have just *these* laws rather than other ones? I want an *explanation* of why they are as they are." I must confess here, as an autobiographical remark, that I cannot help sharing this feeling; I want to ask why the laws of nature, being contingent, are as

---

[6] Garrigou-Lagrange, *God*, I, 254.

155

they are, even though I cannot conceive of what an explanation of this would be like, and even though by my own argument above the request for such an explanation is self-contradictory." [7]

When we come to a place where higher-level explanation stops (some law in physics that we take rightly or wrongly to be basic), we have to say, "That is just the way things are." We may be content to say that no further explanation is needed, or we may (it is a matter of temperament) feel dissatisfied with a bare contingency. Can we end instead with something having its own peculiar necessity free of conceptual muddle? I think we can. There will be those who will be dissatisfied with anything that does not exceed understanding. They were dealt with in the preceding chapter. It is my task to give all the meaning I can to the notion of a necessary being.

Let us suppose a being of the following sort:

1. A being for whose existence nothing else need exist.

2. A being that has always existed.

3. A being upon whom everything else depends for its existence.

One can even have a kind of verification procedure for such qualities. For (1) take away all other things and the being would remain in existence. For (3) take away the being and everything else would pass out of existence. For (2) at *any* time in the past this being could be observed to exist.

If there was such a being, its existence would be necessary in two ways.

*a*) It would not be contingent (*this* sense of "contingent" has to do with things and not propositions); that is, it would not be causally dependent upon anything else for its existence. Necessity here comes to cosmic self-sufficiency.

*b*) Its existence would be necessary for the existence of any-

---

[7] John Hospers, "What is Explanation?" in A. G. N. Flew, ed., *Essays in Conceptual Analysis* (London: MacMillan & Co., 1956), pp. 116–117.

thing else. We may ask, "Why is there such a being?" and we can answer, "Since there was no time at which this being came into existence and since it in no way depends upon anything else for its existence, the question has no point." This being would provide us with an excellent cosmological stopping place. Personally, I should be satisfied with less.

So far, this being could be a star—a very important star, of course—and it would be a matter of investigation to find out what it was about its composition and its relation to other things that allowed it to have the wonderful qualities listed above. If we wanted this being to be God, then among other things we should have to say that it was conscious and created everything else according to its purpose. We should have to say that it was all-wise, all-good, and all-powerful. Yet, even with all of these qualities, the necessity of this being would be such that:

*a*) This being exists, but it is conceivable that it should not have existed.

*b*) This being exists and it is conceivable that it will cease to exist.

The question "Why is there anything at all?" may be asked in such a way that the answer is to be in terms of something that is not merely a matter of how the world in fact is but rather of something that *must* be and *could* not be different. Even our self-sufficient being did not *have* to exist, and if it had not existed there might have been a world similar to this that was dependent upon another or upon no self-sufficient entity, or perhaps there might have been nothing at all. Of course, if there is such a self-sufficient, all-sustaining being, you cannot subtract it from the world without subtracting all other things as well. Thus the old theological slogan:

God — the world = God.
The world — God = Nothing.

But it does not follow from this that if this self-sufficient being had not existed there would have been no other sort of world or that the nonexistence of such a being is inconceivable or that its existence is anything more than a fact about how things happen to be.

For many, God's existence must be logically necessary, though perhaps self-evident only to the infinite intellect. That is, the truth of the proposition "God exists" should be logically necessary. This, indeed, would put God outside of the world of fact and indeed of the world of possibility.

One of the basic ways in which one comes to acquire the concept of a necessary proposition is to learn that a necessary proposition is true in all conceivable states of affairs. No matter what were the case or not the case, the truth of a necessary proposition would be secure. Now, it seems to me that a possible state of affairs is that there should be nothing. But if this state of affairs obtained, the proposition "God exists" would be false. Therefore "God exists" cannot be a necessary proposition. Opposition to this argument must take the form of showing the statement "There was and will be nothing" to be either meaningless or self-contradictory. But this would result in showing the statement "There was and will be something" to be either meaningless or tautological. In fact, *just* so far as I can understand what it is for a thing, *any* thing, to exist, just so far do I understand what it is for it not to exist.

If God's existence, then, cannot be logically necessary, let it be necessary in the ways that I have made clear. Such a necessary being would explain much. Once the notion of such a being is made clear, our philosophical work is at an end. The question whether this being exists will then arise. Against those for whom the existence of this being would be an article of faith, I have no argument.

## "Why is there anything?"

### III

It is time now to ask a question that has been in the background of this whole discussion: "Can science or anything explain everything?" This is really an amalgam of questions, and my answer, as might be expected, is "Yes and no."

1. The question can be answered "Yes" if it is interpreted to mean, "Can there be an explanation, comprising one or many laws, such that from those laws and with the provision of certain relevant matter-of-fact information *any* happening in the world may be predicted?" Whether in the nature of the world such basic laws could be formulated, I do not know. It seems to me probable that they could. And even if the world is not like this, it is not meaningless to suppose it to be so. If someone were to object that "what explains everything explains nothing," I think this would amount to the expression of a silly dogma. I am not suggesting that any set of laws could be employed to explain anything that *could* happen. This indeed would be vacuous.

If everything is to be explained in terms of God's will, then "All things happen and are sustained by God's will" [8] is a basic law. And from this law and information concerning God's will any happening in the world may be predicted. Once again, to save this explanation from vacuity it cannot be employed to explain anything that *could* happen. That is, the explanation would cease to hold if God willed something to happen and it regularly failed to happen.

2. The question can be answered "No" if it is interpreted to mean, "Can there be an explanation of why *all* formulable and mutually consistent explanations (that do in fact hold concerning how the world goes) do in fact hold?" Any such proposed explanation would itself require or not require explanation. If it

---

[8] I am not here concerned with the exceptions supposedly allowed by God, namely, free acts of free agents.

required explanation, it would require something to explain why it itself held as an explanation. If it did not require explanation, there would be one explanation whose application to the world was unexplained. To say that it is self-explanatory is just to say that it requires or has no explanation. The fact that an ultimate explanation, theistic or nontheistic, holds is not a fact to be explained. We come, indeed, to say, "That is just the way things are."

Two points of the greatest importance to theistic forms of explanation may be made here.

*a*) It may be claimed that the world has come to be and is sustained by the will of God and that the natural order of things is ordained by God. The laws of nature are *all* supposed to be devised by and under the control of the will of God. But this *cannot* be true. *There is one law of nature or one way of the world that would be beyond the power of God, namely, that the world should in fact go according to the will of God.* God cannot ordain or will that his ordinations and will are effective. That God's will is effective is just a fact (though a basic one) about how things happen. To ask why God's will is effective is to invite the answer "That is just the way things are." In this way a nontheistic basic law (or set of laws) of nature formulated by physics and a theistic basic law ("All things happen and are sustained by God's will") are not different from one another. To ask "Why?" of either is to invite the same answer. Indeed, this is the final answer to the persistent question "Why?" no matter what form of ultimate explanation we may devise. It would be a pity if the theologian were to allow himself to think of this as a limitation of God's power, because it appears to be logically inevitable.

*b*) The point above is relevant to the feeling (a feeling that helps to incline people to favor theistic hypotheses) that one cannot satisfactorily rest with an ultimate explanation that merely describes how things happen as they do. It is the feeling that the only satisfactory ultimate explanation is of a purposive kind. Those who do not share this feeling may consider it to be purely arbitrary. But a more serious criticism can be made of it than that.

When we ask why things happen in accordance with God's purpose, we get the answer "That is just how things are." That is, this purposive explanation ultimately comes and *must* come to a description of how things happen. The "Why?" of God's purpose rests upon the descriptive "How?" When [9] God acts in such a way [10] that it is true to say he willed something to happen and it happens and it would not have happened but for God's act of will, then this is just a fact about how things happen as they do.

3. The question "Can science or anything explain *everything?*" can be answered "No" if it is interpreted to mean, "Can any one explanation perform every kind of explanatory function?" It is sometimes remarked with more than a little satisfaction that "science does not, cannot, explain everything." The truth in this does not open the way to *mystique* and obscurantism.

When I explain why a tumbler of water fell by saying that a particular person is clumsy, I am not interested in the complicated physiological explanation of why he behaved as he did. I am primarily interested in making reference to the complex pattern of his behavior that warrants me in calling him clumsy and in relating what has just happened to that pattern. This behavioral or macroscopic explanation is logically irreducible to the physiological explanation. I mean simply that the physiological explanation could conceivably have been different from

---

[9] It may be said that God's act of will is timeless and eternal and beyond all comprehension. But what has been said here? God is made to look uncomfortably like a timeless law of nature whose precise formulation we do not understand.

[10] Considering God's nature, it is certainly far from clear what this "way" would be.

what it was, and this would in no way affect the behavioral explanation. From this it does not follow that there is no true and complete physiological explanation of this person's clumsiness.

We can get the same sort of thing within science. Geometrical optics is logically irreducible to physical optics. Explanations in geometrical optics can (conceivably but not in fact) hold whether the physical optics explanation holds or does not hold. From this it does not follow that there is no true and complete physical optics explanation.

Some macroscopic explanations of events are of such emotional value and interest to us that we may irrationally be inclined to reject any scientific form of explanation of those events. When I explain the action of a person by saying "He loves her," I am making reference to the complex pattern of his behavior and feelings that warrants me in saying that he is in love, and I am relating what he has done to that pattern. This explanation can (conceivably) hold no matter what is true of his physiological mechanism. Once again, it does not follow that his action cannot be given a physiological explanation.

Note that the macroscopic patterns [11] are logically primary, for they are what we mean by "clumsiness," "love," "fragility." We correlate patterns revealed by scientific techniques to them and not vice versa. Their interest, meaning, and logical independence cannot be reduced away. A scientific form of explanation tells us how, even in its intimate recesses, the world is ordered. It does not and cannot replace or supplant other forms of explanation.

The same is true of a theistic form of explanation. A theistic explanation may tell us how the world is ordered—it is ordered by the command of God.

---

[11] I would want to include here an indefinite number of items, e.g., economic, historical, aesthetic, and political explanations.

### "Why is there anything?"

The macroscopic forms of explanation (and in this context, the scientific forms of explanation would have to be included as well) could (conceivably) hold whether the theistic explanation holds or not or whether or not the details of its valid formulation vary from one time to another.

A basic law of physics or a basic law about how the world's creation and sustenance is by God's will are neither of them adequate for the deduction of every form of explanation by which in irreducible and various ways we organize and order features of the world's activity.

# Conclusion

RELIGION is much more than poetry, but it is poetry. Religious writings, ritual, and ceremonial behavior are most richly emotionally evocative. Religion is much more than a way of life, but it is a way of living. It is, at the least, to play the life-and-death game of acting and living as if by the will of another—"I live, yet no longer I, but Christ in me." Religion is much more than a way of seeing the world, but it is this. There is an easy economy that comes from organizing features in the world within us and outside us as the activity of God or Satan. So much we have, and so much we are slow to lose.

But religion is more than these, and we have inquired what more it is. For all of these things could be true and valuable and there be no God. That is, we needed the added claim that there is a Being who created us and the world, who sustains us all, and who will bring us finally to judgment. I have tried to show how the concept of such a Being may carry with it no confusion or obscurity. But then such a concept makes God not sufficiently

164

# Conclusion

beyond our understanding to be worthy of religious awe. And here we come to another service of religion. It brings to order and focal point by means of a form of language, life, and ceremony our many feelings of mystery and of wonder and awe and helplessness at the workings of the world. Yet in the provision of this service religion lays itself open to philosophical criticism.

If religion limited itself to the assertion that there are things beyond our knowing and understanding, it would be compatible with atheism. It is no answer to us for the theologian to claim that he knows and understands in part but not in full. We have found difficulties in the part that he claims to understand. Further, he must answer the challenge that the remainder (that passeth his understanding) cannot form a part of his belief or faith.

That which is beyond our understanding is not, however, entirely formless. In a way, the religious man and the atheist are in a kind of disagreement even here. The void is formed for the religious man by a direction of life and inquiry which the atheist does not share. There is no saying where that inquiry ends. The Christian does not see beyond the mind's eye, yet he looks and sets his eye where the unbeliever does not—he looks to Christ.

Man will ever look in directions beyond his vision. The propriety of this enterprise, however, entails no justification of theological obscurities and no assurance that a saving explication by someone, sometime, somehow is possible. Indeed, the argument of this book would suggest that to hope for such explication, by human or other means, is irrational.

# Index

167

# Index